MODERN RAINBOW

14 Imaginative Quilts that Play with Color

REBECCA BRYAN

STASH BOOKS®

an imprint of C&T Publishing

PUBLISHER: Amy Marson

CREATIVE DIRECTOR: Gailen Runge

ART DIRECTOR: Kristy Zacharias

EDITORS: Liz Aneloski and Lee Jonsson

TECHNICAL EDITORS: Julie Waldman and Ann Haley

COVER/BOOK DESIGNER: April Mostek

PRODUCTION COORDINATORS: Rue Flaherty and Freesia Pearson Blizard

PRODUCTION EDITOR: Katie Van Amburg

ILLUSTRATORS: Wendy Mathson and Rebecca Bryan

PHOTO ASSISTANT: Mary Peyton Peppo

STYLE PHOTOGRAPHY by Nissa Brehmer; **INSTRUCTIONAL PHOTOGRAPHY** by Diane Pedersen, unless otherwise noted

Published by Stash Books, an imprint of C&T Publishing, Inc., P.O. Box 1456, Lafayette, CA 94549

Library of Congress Cataloging-in-Publication Data

Bryan, Rebecca, 1980-

Modern rainbow : 14 imaginative quilts that play with color / Rebecca Bryan.

    pages cm

ISBN 978-1-61745-018-1 (softcover)

1. Quilting. 2. Quilting--Patterns. 3. Quilts. 4. Color in textile crafts. I. Title.

TT835.B758 2015

746.46--dc23

          2014029601

Printed in China

10 9 8 7 6 5 4 3 2 1

CONTENTS

PROJECTS

DEDICATION

To my God for giving me the dream
and the faith to see it through.

To my mother for teaching me how.

To my husband for encouraging me.

To my children for the future.

And to my Savior for redeeming me.

"Many waters cannot quench love."
—Song of Solomon 8:7

ACKNOWLEDGMENTS

Thank you to my family and friends for your love and encouragement, support, and prayers. Your prayers mean so much to me. Thank you!

Thank you to the staff at C&T for this opportunity and for working with me along this journey.

Thank you to my quilty friends, near and far, who show tremendous versatility and creativity every day! You guys are amazing and so inspiring.

Thank you to Angela Walters for (beautifully!) quilting some of my quilts.

Thank you to the Warm Company, which provided the Warm & White batting; Aurifil, which provided thread; and Robert Kaufman Fabrics for providing the fabric for the solid rainbow swatches.

And lastly, thank you for reading my book.

PREFACE

Quilting with rainbow colors combines two things I love dearly: sewing and color.

I am fortunate to have grown up in a family heavily endowed with creative spirits. My grandfather built a sturdy boathouse. My stepfather tinkers. My father created a bountiful garden. One day my dad even surprised me by painting a mean landscape. The women of the family, my great-grandmothers and grandmothers, were quilters.

My mother taught me the art of sewing and quilting as I grew. But I didn't become serious about sewing until after I was married. It was then I discovered vibrant, modern-colored fabrics. It was the colors that inspired me to refine my sewing skills and to design and make quilts.

I love laying out fabrics, rearranging them until the colors almost shine. And I love anything arranged in color order. Rainbows themselves are great, but office supplies in color order? Swoon. Books arranged in color order? Swoon. Fabric in color order? Double swoon!

Perhaps my love of rainbows started with the popular 80s doll Rainbow Brite. My favorite kindergarten friend gave me a Rainbow Brite doll for my sixth birthday. I remember how her rainbow-colored sleeves shone in sunny, sparkly goodness. It was a good day.

Even now, I can hardly resist anything that's in color order. Surely I can't be the only one who ogles merchandise arranged by color. Be it colored pencils, bowls, paint chips, scarves, or fabric, if it is arranged by color, it might just wind up in my shopping cart. I think it's a marketing trick.

I am tremendously inspired by the colors of the rainbow. They hold such possibility. The start of a new school year, the start of a closet, organized. A new drawing or a new quilt waits beyond those colored pencils and fabric. Colors in rainbow order awaken a sense of creativity for me, and I hope I can share this love with you.

INTRODUCTION

After covering some color basics, I will show you different ways to manipulate the spectrum. My hope is that you find some ideas that develop your natural sense of color and help you create your own unique spectrum.

Classic rainbow colors are great, but I wanted to create spectrums that challenge the rainbow cliché. As fashion and design and culture change from year to year, so do the popular colors. New colors can breathe life into a tired rainbow.

I designed the quilts included in this book to showcase a spectrum of color. I wanted to make quilts that were easy but also challenging in terms of both skill and design.

I love many types of quilting styles, so the patterns are divided into these categories: modern traditional, modern, and improvisational and liberated. Each of these categories has its own approach to quiltmaking. Be sure to read each section's introduction for special tips.

I have invested much work to ensure the accuracy of the patterns, but it's always a great idea to read the entire pattern before beginning and, where applicable, make a test block.

And one last note: as much as I love colors in color order, I actually just love color. So yes, these quilts would look great in other color stories, too!

Enjoy!

THE BASICS

USING THE SPECTRUM IN QUILTS

This chapter will cover some basics of color theory and show ways to manipulate colors to create a unique rainbow color story.

DEFINING THE SPECTRUM

We have all seen the spectrum. Maybe in a rainbow arcing the sky? Perhaps you studied the spectrum in school, in science or art classes. Isn't it interesting that these diverse subjects can cover the same topic?

Primary, Secondary, and Tertiary Colors

Simply put, the rainbow consists of ordered colors. There are many ways to visualize the rainbow, but typically in sewing and quilting, we refer to a color wheel.

Looking at the color wheel, we see that the *primary* colors—blue, red, and yellow—when combined, form the *secondary* colors—purple (red + blue), orange (red + yellow), and green (yellow + blue). *Tertiary* colors—blue-purple,

red-purple, red-orange, yellow-orange, yellow-green, and blue-green—are created when a primary and secondary color blend or when two secondary colors blend.

Sprinkled throughout this book, you will find different rainbow color stories. There are classic rainbows and variations. I hope you can find some color inspiration there as well. Have fun!

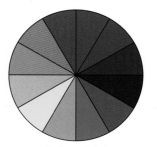

Color wheel

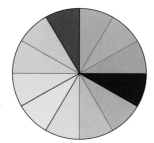

Primary colors

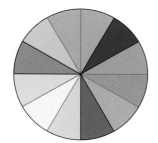

Secondary colors

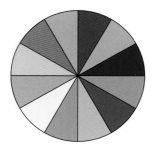

Tertiary colors

Warm and Cool

The rainbow is composed of warm and cool colors.

Warm colors include the energetic side of the color wheel: red, orange, yellow, and their variations. Think red lipstick and red shoes, vibrant fall leaves and fresh-squeezed orange juice, warm sunshine, and a crackling fire. Warm colors seem as though they are coming toward the viewer.

Cool colors include the more subdued colors: green, blue, purple, and their variations. Think purple tulips or a tropical beach, an iceberg or crisp blue sky, green apples or lush green grass. Cool colors seem to recede from the viewer.

Color Defined

A hue is a color.

A tint occurs when white is added to a color. Pastels are tints.

When black is added to a color, it produces a shade.

A tone results when gray is added to a color.

Chroma is the purity of a color. A color in its purest form, without black, white, or gray, possesses a high chroma.

Volume refers to how saturated in color a fabric is. A high-volume fabric is saturated with color and a low-volume fabric is very light.

WORKING WITH DIFFERENT TYPES
of Fabrics

Identifying a fabric's color is essential if we are to arrange fabrics in color order. Let's consider hue to be the fabric's core color and the twelve colors in the color wheel (page 10) as the twelve basic hues.

We might consider the fabric shop to be our crayon box and the fabrics, our crayons. Fortunately, there is a plethora of fabric out there for us! In a well-rounded fabric stash, it's good to have many choices within each of the twelve basic colors. Having many fabrics will give you more choices in color, tint, tone, or saturation as you choose fabrics for a rainbow quilt.

Solid-Color Fabrics

Solids are an easy basic. They are simple to arrange in color order and are widely available in many tints and shades. To make the perfect color easier to identify, manufacturers offer color cards, which show samples of each solid color offered—similar to paint chips.

Solids in color order

Single-Color Fabrics

With tone-on-white and tone-on-tone fabrics, we can easily identify the colors and sort them into color order.

Tone-on-white fabrics have a color printed on a white background.

Tone-on-white fabrics

Tone-on-tone fabrics have shades, tints, or tones of the same color. But the colors are still readily identifiable and the fabrics can be easily sorted into color order.

Tone-on-tone fabrics in color order

Multicolored Fabrics

Identifying a fabric's color and proper spectrum placement gets trickier as additional color accents are added to it. Fabrics that have analogous colors as accents are easier to sort. Analogous colors are colors next to each other on the color wheel. Here's an example of multicolored fabrics sorted by color.

Multicolored fabrics in color order

The addition of accent colors can make the fabric's color read differently to the viewer. Thus, multicolored fabrics can be useful as tertiary colors (page 10) that create color transitions and bring depth of color.

Multicolored fabric used as a tertiary yellow-orange

CUSTOMIZING YOUR RAINBOW

Who we are as people affects how we perceive and choose color. Whether your color sense comes naturally or has been cultivated, you have at least some color intuition. Let's explore ways to choose colors and fabrics that bring a unique rainbow color story to a quilt.

Circular or Linear Spectrum

Does the quilt pattern call for a circular or linear spectrum? If the pattern calls for a circular spectrum, the entire spectrum will need to transition from each color to the next.

For example, *Huckleberry* (page 64) calls for fabrics to be arranged in a *circular spectrum*. The tertiary colors throughout are used to carry the movement of color through the entire circle of color.

For a *linear spectrum*, the first and last colors don't need a transition because they will never meet. The colors for *Icarus Star* (page 107) can be linear. The first and last colors (purple and orange) do not meet, so no color transition is necessary between them.

Contrast

Contrast is how different the fabrics look when shown in close proximity to each other. You can increase or decrease contrast by manipulating the color, tint, shade, and tone of the fabrics. A general rule of thumb is this: To decrease contrast, use more colors or fabrics. To increase contrast, use fewer colors or fabrics.

CONTRAST WITHIN THE SPECTRUM

You can play with contrast within the spectrum. For example, *Bubbles* (page 39) uses only five colors—red, orange, yellow, green, and blue. But to soften the contrast, I used a few different fabrics within each color.

By using more fabrics to represent the spectrum, one can almost create a seamless spectrum, as the colors gradually transition from one to another across the quilt. *Rainbow Streak* (page 51) uses six main colors. To move the quilt from color to color, I chose six different fabrics for each color, each slightly different from the next.

CONTRAST BETWEEN THE FOREGROUND AND BACKGROUND

Think about the contrast between the foreground and the background. You can decrease the contrast by choosing a few different white background fabrics rather than just one. I've applied this concept in *Wavelength* (page 88).

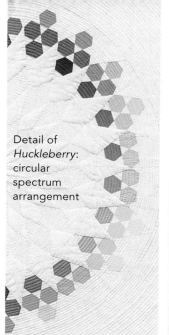

Detail of *Huckleberry*: circular spectrum arrangement

Detail of *Icarus Star*: linear spectrum arrangement

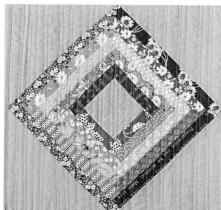

Detail of *Bubbles*: contrast within the spectrum

Detail of *Rainbow Streak*: seamless spectrum

Detail of *Wavelength*: contrast between the foreground and background

BEYOND THE RAINBOW CLICHÉ

Let's discuss ways to go beyond the rainbow cliché.

Use Neutrals

Adding neutrals is an option for giving a rainbow color scheme a slightly different look, especially if the colors become overwhelming. I love lots of color, so I tend to gravitate toward high-volume, saturated palettes when I choose fabrics.

Low-volume neutrals

Neutrals provide a *negative space*—the space around the intended subject in a painting, a photo, or a quilt.

Use the Colors Out of Order

I love to add an element of surprise in my quilts. While you could arrange the fabrics strictly by color order, sometimes it's fun to subtly rearrange the order. The element of surprise keeps the viewer's eyes moving. My favorite ways to create some chaos are to vary the saturation, value, or tint, or to subtly rearrange a tertiary color or two.

Rainbow Remix (page 95) offers a rainbow that's not in color order. The slightly out-of-order colors provide contrast and keep the viewer's eye moving across the quilt.

Detail of *Rainbow Remix*: rainbow not in color order

Use Other Palettes

Beyond the classic rainbow, there are many color palettes we could explore; for example, pastels, jewel tones, or neons. We could use a rainbow within one or two colors, such as a palette moving from blue-green to green to green-yellow.

Detail of *Ducks in a Row*: dropping a color from rainbow palette

Omit Colors

Dropping a color or two from the rainbow palette will give the rainbow a different look. It won't scream "I'm a rainbow!" or "I like rainbows!" *Ducks in a Row* (page 79) leaves out the colors red, red-purple, purple, blue-purple, and blue.

Use Your Favorite Colors

Another option would be to use more of your favorite colors in the rainbow. Although I claim not to have a favorite color, I found myself reaching for jewel tones, especially purple, teal, and citron, as I built the color stories for the quilts in this book. Absolutely, use more of your favorite colors. Start with your favorites and build a rainbow color story around them.

WHERE TO FIND COLOR INSPIRATION

- Look at your favorite blogs, magazines, or catalogs for the latest colors.

- Observe trending colors; they change as fashion trends change.

- Go to the paint store and gather paint-sample chips.

- Look at new fabric collections. (Although buying new fabric is an option, you don't necessarily have to.)

- Look to your stash and pull out fabrics that match the trending colors; then arrange them in color order.

- Choose your favorite multicolored fabric from your stash. Look at its selvage, where you will find little colored dots. Use these colors as inspiration.

Selvage-inspired color story

TOOLS AND MATERIALS

This section covers the basic tools used in quiltmaking. Although these tools are an investment, most usually last awhile. Typically, you can find each of these products at a local quilt shop or craft store.

ROTARY CUTTER AND SELF-HEALING MAT

A 45mm rotary cutter is a standard tool for easy cutting. Replace the blade as it becomes dull. Gridded cutting mats come in several sizes and colors. Get as large a mat as you have space for.

CLEAR, ACRYLIC GRIDDED RULERS

Acrylic rulers come in a variety of sizes, but the two rulers I use most are 6″ × 24″ and 6″ × 12″. Get a ruler with a minimum of ⅛″ grids and marks for 15°, 30°, 45°, and 60° angles.

SCISSORS

Invest in a few good pairs of scissors. I keep a small pair to snip thread, a pair of Gingher knife-edge scissors for cutting fabric, and a pair for paper cutting.

STRAIGHT PINS AND PINCUSHIONS

Pinning layers of fabric or blocks together is essential for accuracy. Fine, glass-head pins work well and tend not to mar the fabric. Lovely pincushions are, well, lovely. Can one ever have too many?

PRESSER FEET

For the projects in this book you will need a regular presser foot, a walking foot, and a darning or free-motion foot. I also recommend a ¼″ foot to aid in piecing accuracy.

IRON AND IRONING BOARD

An iron that can give a sharp press is essential. Look for an iron with adjustable steam. A large, broad ironing board is ideal for pressing large pieces. A small ironing board is nice for pressing small pieces.

SEAM RIPPER

I wish it weren't the case, but sometimes mistakes are made. Buy a seam ripper. Sigh.

MARKING TOOLS

My two favorite tools for fabric marking are my water-soluble, fine-tip fabric-marking pen and a Hera marker, which creases the fabric.

HAND-SEWING NEEDLES

The projects in this book call for two types of needles: sharps for attaching the quilt binding by hand and crewel needles for hand quilting with perle cotton thread.

BASTING TOOLS

When preparing a quilt top for quilting, at the very minimum you will need blue painter's tape and curved quilter's safety pins. The

curve in the safety pin helps pick up all three layers in the quilt sandwich. A Kwik Klip can protect your fingers when pin basting. If you want to spray baste, you will need at least one can of quality basting spray.

TEMPLATE MATERIAL

To make sturdy templates, you will need template plastic or thin cardboard (for example, from a cereal box).

THIMBLE

A thimble of the proper size can protect fingers when you are working by hand.

BATTING

I typically use a single layer of batting in my quilts. I love Warm & White batting because it's readily available and I can usually buy it in bulk and on sale.

THREAD

Quality thread is essential when piecing and quilting. In general, my machine and I prefer 100% cotton Aurifil threads.

HAND-QUILTING THREAD

I can't get enough of hand quilting using perle cotton thread. It comes in three sizes: 5, 8, and 12. The lower the number, the thicker the thread.

TECHNIQUES AND SEWING BASICS

PREPARING FABRICS

Prewash or jump right in? Whether you prewash your fabrics or not is your choice. Either way has its merits. Prewashing gives an added layer of protection against fabric bleeding and excessive shrinking. Jumping right in allows for, well, jumping right in! Either way, fabric requirements for the projects in this book assume a usable fabric width of 40″ after removing the selvages.

ROTARY CUTTING

Squaring Up the Fabric

Prior to cutting, it is important to square up the fabric. This process ensures you are cutting fabric-width strips that are straight. Refold the fabric in half, with wrong sides together, matching the selvages. Smooth the fabric until it folds evenly, even if the cut edges no longer align. If necessary, iron the fabric.

Lay the fabric on the cutting mat, lining up the fold with a horizontal line on the mat. Then use a vertical line on the mat to trim the fabric edge by aligning the side of a long acrylic ruler (a 6″ × 24″ ruler is useful here) with that same vertical line. Cut along that vertical line with a rotary cutter.

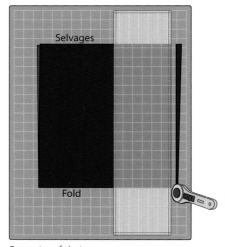

Squaring fabric

Cutting Strips by Fabric Width

Fabric width is the measurement of fabric from selvage to selvage. The usable width is the measurement after the selvages have been removed.

To cut strips from the fabric width:

1. Square up the fabric (page 18). Then realign the fold with a horizontal line and the freshly cut edge with a vertical line on the gridded cutting mat.

2. Align the long edge of a 6″ × 24″ acrylic ruler with a vertical line on the mat to match the desired strip width (for example, 2½″).

3. Then, with the rotary cutter in your dominant hand and your other hand firmly holding the ruler in place, glide the rotary blade along the side of the ruler. (Always cut along the side of your dominant hand.)

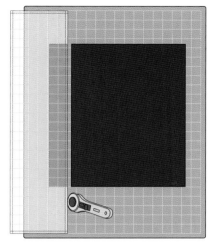

Cutting strips × fabric width

Cutting at an Angle

Several patterns in this book call for cutting fabric or strip sets at an angle. Typically, each cutting mat and acrylic ruler will have marks for 30°, 45°, and 60° angles. To cut angled pieces and units, simply line up the fabric or unit on a gridded cutting mat. Line up the desired angle on the acrylic ruler to either a fabric edge or a line on the cutting mat. (How you line up the angles and to what line will depend on the desired shape.) Then make your cut.

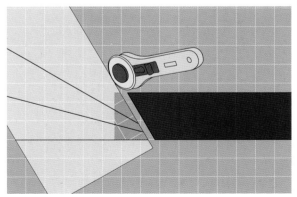

Cutting at an angle

Cutting Diamonds

To cut a diamond:

1. Cut a strip from the fabric width as indicated by the pattern; for example, cut a strip 2½″ × fabric width.

2. Cut one end of the fabric strip at the angle indicated by the pattern. For example, cut the strip at 60° (see Cutting at an Angle, page 19).

3. Turn the acrylic ruler so that it is parallel with the first cut. Measure the width from the first cut as indicated by the pattern. In our example, measure 2½″ from the first cut and make a second cut to finish cutting the diamond.

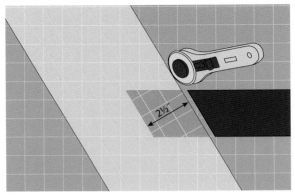

Cutting a diamond

Cutting Angled Units

Some patterns call for an angled unit (such as a strip, unit, or strip set) to be cut to a specific length. In general:

1. Make the initial angled cut (see Cutting at an Angle, page 19).

2. You can either use your ruler as a guide in Steps 2 and 3, or use the lines on your cutting mat as a guide. Turn the acrylic ruler parallel to the cut, or align the cut to the gridded cutting mat.

3. Use the ruler or gridded cutting mat to measure the desired distance away from the first cut. Line up the ruler and cut.

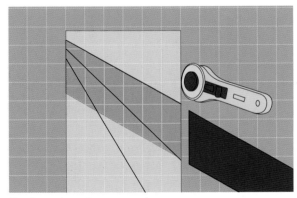

Cutting a length at an angle

USING A DESIGN WALL
for Color Placement and Quilt Layout

A flat surface is a must when laying out pieces or blocks in quilting. Ideally, a permanent design wall in your quilting studio works best. You can leave your units there to ponder color placement and world peace. However, if you don't have that luxury—and I don't—a clean floor works well for laying out units, although it affords less time for pondering. But snapping a picture works well too.

TEMPLATES

Three quilts in this book have templates (*Lucy in the Sky*, page 32, *Huckleberry*, page 64, and *Ducks in a Row*, page 79).

Making Templates

From the patterns (pullout pages P1 and P2), cut out, trace, or make a copy of the pattern. If you are using template plastic for the templates, you can trace the template directly onto the plastic. If you are using poster board or thin cardboard, paste a paper template onto the cardboard and then cut it out.

On each template, you can punch a small hole at the match points (page 22) by using a 1/8" hole punch or an awl. Then, with a sharp pencil, you can easily mark the match points on the wrong side of the fabric.

Using the Templates to Cut Pattern Pieces

To cut pattern pieces using templates, first cut strips from the fabric width as indicated in the project instructions. Use the template to trace the pattern pieces on the strip with a fabric-marking pen. Then use the acrylic ruler and rotary cutter to cut along the traced lines.

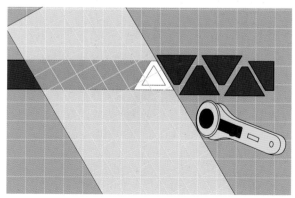

Using templates

SEWING BASICS

Pinning

Before sewing two pieces together, it is a good idea to first pin them together.

1. With right sides together, first pin the aligning seams. Pin through the fabric on either side of the seam.

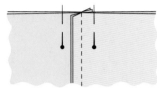

Pinning nested seams

2. Pin the start and end of the stitching line.

3. If you want, pin some more between the center and sides.

When pinning rows together, follow the same general process. Align and pin the center units. Then align and pin the units at either end. Then align and pin the units between the sides and center. Then pin as needed to ease any extra fabric between units.

Match Points

When sewing pieces with angles other than 90°, pin the match points. The match points are where seamlines intersect. Where applicable, match points have been indicated on patterns.

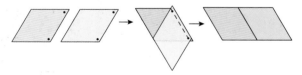

Match points.

Machine Sewing

SEAM ALLOWANCES

The width between the sewn seam and the raw edge of the fabric is called the seam allowance. Unless otherwise indicated in the instructions, all seam allowances are a scant ¼˝.

SEWING CURVES

Piecing curves can be intimidating, but with plenty of pins and some patience it is doable.

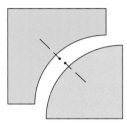

Curved pieces with midpoints marked

1. Fold the units in half and place a pin at the midpoint of each curve. With right sides together, pin the midpoints together. Then pin the match points at either end. Then pin generously between the match points and the midpoint, easing in the fabric of the concave piece to the convex piece.

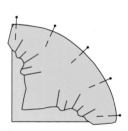

Pinning curves

2. Stitch slowly, using a scant ¼˝ seam allowance.

3. Press the seam open or toward the concave piece.

Finished curved seam

Sewing Strip Sets

Strip sewing is such a handy technique. Here is the general process for sewing strip sets, along with some tips.

1. Cut the fabric into strips as directed in the project instructions. For example, cut strips 2½″ × fabric width.

2. Sew the strips right sides together, then press. An easy way to do this is to sew pairs of strips together. Then sew the pairs together into units of 4, 6, and so on, depending on the instructions.

3. To cut strip sets, lay the strip set on the cutting mat, aligning it with the grid. Square up one end of the strip set the same way you squared up your fabric before cutting (see Preparing Fabrics, page 18).

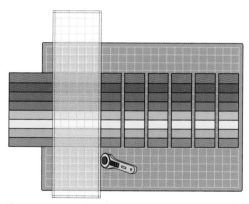

Square strip sets, then measure and cut strips.

4. Cut straight or angled strips as directed by the project instructions.

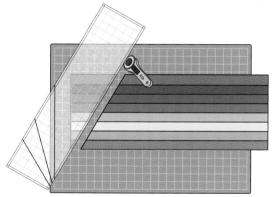

Cut angled strip sets.

(see Preparing Fabrics, page 18)

For sewing and cutting accurate strip sets:

- Shorten the sewing machine's stitch length to prevent cut strips from coming apart. (I shorten mine from 2.7 to 2.3.)

- Press seams open to prevent the set from warping.

- Press seams after sewing a few strips instead of waiting until all strips are sewn.

- Sew the seams in alternating directions to prevent warping (sew in one direction, and then for the next seam, flip the set and sew in the opposite direction).

- Instead of working with strip sets that are fabric width (40″), it may be easier to work with smaller strip sets. Cut each strip in half so it is half the fabric width (around 20″). Before you do this, be sure to check the project instructions to make sure that your shorter strips will work, and double the number of strip sets you make!

Pressing

Pressing versus ironing is key. Remember—iron your clothes; press your quilt blocks. While ironing is a back-and-forth motion, pressing is a lift up, set down, lift up, set down action.

There are two ways one can press a seam. Some quilters prefer pressing seams to the side; others prefer pressing the seam open. Both ways have their merits.

Where possible, I like to nest my seams. When I want to decrease bulk at the seam, I press the seam open. Instructions in the book will reflect these preferences.

Here's the general process:

1. Set the seam by laying the sewn unit on the ironing board and pressing the seam briefly.

2. Open the sewn unit and set it right side down on the ironing board. Finger-press the seam open or to the side (as indicated by the project instructions or personal preference). Press the seam by lifting and lowering the iron.

3. Turn the sewn unit over—right side up—and press again.

Dog-Ears

When irregularly shaped pieces are sewn together, bits of fabric stick out after pressing. These bits of fabric are called "dog-ears." Trim the dog-ears to decrease fabric bulk.

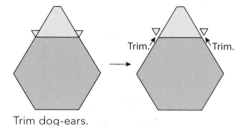

Trim dog-ears.

Squaring Up Blocks

When quilt tops are pieced from blocks, the blocks should be ½˝ larger than the finished block size. It's important to make sure all the blocks are approximately the same size. Using a cutting mat, an acrylic ruler, and a rotary cutter, trim each block to the size stated in the project instructions.

Appliqué

In this book two projects require you to appliqué a six-pointed star onto a wholecloth background. I can't imagine needle-turning such giant pieces, so I contrived a different way to affix each star to the background.

1. Turn under the edges of the star by ¼˝.

Note: Another option for Step 1 is to place the star right side down on a piece of lightweight interfacing. Stitch all the way around the star, ¼˝ from the edge, leaving a 4˝ space for turning. Trim the seam allowance on the interfacing. Clip the corners and trim the seam allowance at the points, then turn the star right side out and press.

2. Pin the star in place.

3. Topstitch ⅛˝ around the edges of the entire star.

FINISHING THE QUILT

Making the Quilt Back

Instructions call for backings made larger than the finished quilt top by 4″ on each side.

1. Trim the selvages from the backing fabric.

2. Cut the backing fabric into 2 equal widths and sew the pieces together lengthwise to make a backing 8″ larger than the quilt top. Depending on the size of the quilt, sometimes the seam will run vertically on the quilt back and sometimes horizontally.

3. Press the seam open.

Preparing the Batting

Cut a piece of batting that is 8″ wider and 8″ longer than the quilt top.

Making a Quilt Sandwich

Before making the quilt sandwich, press the backing and quilt top. If your batting is wrinkled, put it in the dryer with a damp dishtowel for a few minutes on low heat.

1. Lay the backing material wrong side up on a large, flat surface. Secure the 4 sides and corners of the fabric to the work surface with blue painter's tape. Make sure the material is taut but not stretched.

2. Now lay the batting on top of the backing. Smooth out any wrinkles.

3. Center the quilt top right side up on top of the batting, making sure there is approximately 4″ of batting and backing material on each side. Smooth out the quilt top.

Pin Basting

Using small, curved quilter's safety pins, pin through all of the layers of the quilt sandwich. Pin every 4″–6″, or roughly the width of your hand.

Spray Basting

If you prefer to spray baste the quilt, make the quilt sandwich as usual, then fold back half of the quilt top. Spray the adhesive directly onto the batting as indicated by the manufacturer's instructions. Then carefully unfold that half of the quilt top and smooth it out onto the batting. Repeat with the other half of the quilt top. Finally, repeat the process with the quilt backing by folding the quilt top and batting in half. Make sure to have ventilation and protect other surfaces when using basting spray.

Quilting

Unless indicated, I quilted each quilt on my domestic sewing machine—and you can too.

STRAIGHT-LINE QUILTING

For quilting straight lines, a walking foot is a must. Using a ruler, mark lines on the quilt top using a Hera marker or an erasable marking pen, or use painter's tape. For organic-looking lines, you can eyeball the straight line as you quilt.

FREE-MOTION QUILTING

For free-motion quilting, you will need to adjust your sewing machine. Following the manufacturer's instructions, drop the feed dogs, change the presser foot to the darning or free-motion foot, decrease the foot pressure to 0, and adjust the tension as needed.

For either straight-line or free-motion quilting, you will need to leave long lengths of thread when starting. When you start, place the quilt under the presser foot. Hold the top thread between your fingertips while you needle down and needle up to bring up the bobbin thread. Pull the top thread until the bobbin thread tail comes up. Set both top and bobbin threads to the side, away from where you will be quilting. After you are finished quilting, knot and bury these threads within the batting using a hand-quilting needle, and trim the excess thread. When starting or ending the quilting at the edge of the quilt, just backstitch and clip away excess threads.

HAND QUILTING

In my opinion, nothing beats the feel of a hand-quilted quilt. Hand quilting used to stress me out and depress me because I thought my stitches weren't good enough. Now, I consider hand-quilted stitches to be something like handwriting—everyone has a different, imperfect style. With that new attitude and a little practice, I now love hand quilting.

While my great-grandmother Minnie could get ten tiny, precise stitches to an inch, I use a big pick stitch of roughly three to five stitches to an inch, which is easily achievable using perle embroidery thread.

While some quilters prefer using a hoop, I like to quilt without a hoop so that I can manipulate the fabric around my needle.

1. To start, take about an 18″ length of thread, thread the needle, and knot the end of the thread with a small, one-loop knot.

2. About an inch from where you plan to start quilting, take the needle through the quilt top and batting, but not the backing. Bring the needle and thread back through to the top at the place where you want to start quilting. Bury the knot by gently tugging the thread until the knot pulls through to the batting.

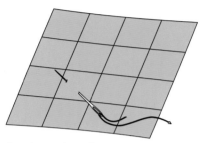
Starting a thread

3. With your dominant hand, insert the needle where you want to start quilting. Bring the needle through all the layers until you feel the tip of the needle with your other hand underneath the quilt. Then rock the needle back through to the quilt top.

4. Rock the needle up and down with a thimbled finger to stack 3–5 stitches on the needle. (With my left hand I manipulate the fabric while I rock the needle.)

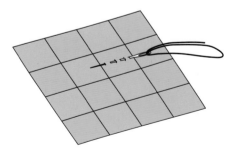
Stacking stitches

5. To finish a thread, make a knot close to the quilt top. Pull it tight. Insert the needle into the hole the thread is coming out of, through

the batting, and up through the top again so that the needle tip sticks out about an inch away. Pull the needle through, and gently pull the knot through the top and the batting. Snip the thread end.

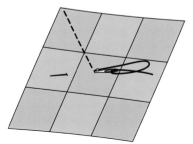

Finishing a thread

SQUARING THE QUILT

Square up the quilt using an acrylic ruler so that the backing and batting are the same size as the quilt top. Use the ruler to ensure the corners are square, or 90°.

Binding the Quilt

The last step in finishing a quilt is attaching the binding, which will finish off the raw edges along the sides. If the quilt has straight sides, use straight-cut binding, but if the quilt has curved or other irregular sides, use bias binding.

STRAIGHT-CUT BINDING

From the binding fabric, cut 2½˝ widths of fabric until you have enough fabric to cover each side of the quilt plus an extra 20˝–30˝ for seaming the strips and joining the ends. Keep in mind that when you join the strips, you will lose 2½˝ with each seam. To figure out how many strips you need, divide the total binding measurement by 40˝.

BIAS BINDING

To make bias binding, cut strips on the bias.

1. From at least ½ yard of fabric, trim the selvages and unfold the fabric. Mark a line at a 45° angle using the 6˝ × 24˝ acrylic ruler, and cut the fabric along that line.

2. Sew the 2 pieces together to form a diamond by stitching the straight edges together. Press the seam open.

3. From this unit, cut 2½˝-wide strips from the 45° cut.

PREPARING A CONTINUOUS BINDING STRIP

1. Join the binding strips by aligning the ends of 2 strips perpendicular to each other and with right sides together. Sew along the diagonal from corner to corner. Trim the seam to ¼˝. Press the seam open.

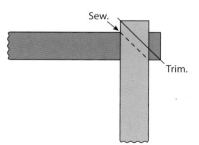

Join strip ends.

2. Repeat this process until all the binding strips are sewn together.

3. With wrong sides together, fold the entire strip in half lengthwise, matching raw ends, and press.

Fold and press binding.

ATTACHING THE BINDING TO THE QUILT

1. Leaving a 6″ length and matching the raw end of the binding strip to the raw edge of the quilt, begin sewing the binding to the quilt using a ¼″ seam allowance. Start in the middle of one side and use a walking foot.

2. Stop sewing ¼″ away from the corner, backstitch, and cut the threads.

End stitching ¼″ from corner.

Start stitching binding.

3. Rotate the quilt to prepare to sew the next side. Fold the binding up at a 45° angle.

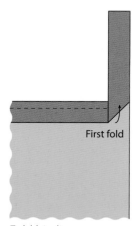

First fold

Fold binding up.

4. Fold the binding back down, keeping the original 45° fold intact and creating a second fold. Align the second fold with the upper edge of the quilt, and the raw edge of the binding with the raw edge of the quilt. Pin in place.

Second fold

Align binding with next side.

5. Starting with a backstitch, sew from the upper edge of the quilt and over the folds.

6. Continue sewing, repeating Steps 2–5 for each corner.

7. Stop about 10″ from the original starting point. Overlap the binding strips by 2½″ and trim excess fabric away.

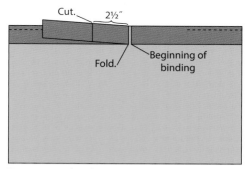

Cut.　2½″

Fold.　Beginning of binding

Trim excess binding.

8. Unfold the binding strips and match right sides together perpendicularly. Pin and sew along the diagonal. Trim the seam allowance to ¼˝ and press the seam open.

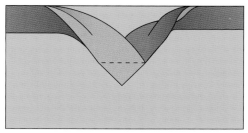

Pin and sew.

9. Refold the binding and finish sewing the binding strip to the quilt.

FINISHING THE BINDING BY HAND

You can finish the binding by hand by wrapping it around to the back of the quilt and using a blind hem stitch to secure it.

FINISHING THE BINDING BY MACHINE

Increasingly, I've been finishing the binding by machine. I've found the best way to do this is to first sew the binding to the *back* of the quilt. Then, working with one side at a time, I wrap the folded edge of the binding strip to the front of the quilt and topstitch ⅛˝ away from the folded edge.

LOVING THE QUILT

Quilts were made to love, so be sure to love that quilt. Let it play with your children and warm you on the couch. Let it hang on your wall or serve as a tablecloth.

Occasionally, the quilt will need a washing. If you didn't prewash your fabrics, prepare for some shrinking. This shrinking will bring out the crinkly goodness of your quilting. But also protect your quilt from color bleeds by throwing some Synthrapol or Shout Color Catchers into the washing machine. Wash it in cold water on the delicate cycle, and hang it to dry or dry it on low heat.

MODERN TRADITIONAL QUILTS

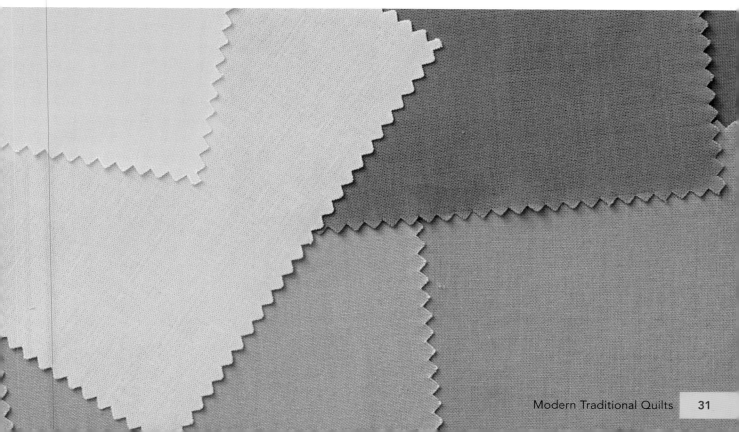

Quilts in this section are directly inspired by traditional quilt patterns. I love traditional quilt patterns!

In piecing quilts such as these, I try to strive for perfection but not to sweat the little mistake here and there. Life's too short!

As I've sewn more and more, I've come to appreciate the imperfection here and there. A misplaced fabric, a missed seam, a "make-do" element: these are all qualities I value in my favorite quilts. They hint at the humanity of the quilter. Was the maker rocking a baby while stitching that seam? Did the fabric run out just before that last block? Was the quilter worried that day?

When making these quilts, I hope you allow your humanity to shine through your imperfections, too. Enjoy!

LUCY IN THE SKY

Quilted by Angela Walters

Many modern quilt designs find their roots in traditional quilting. In this quilt the traditional Ohio Star block frames a paper-pieced rainbow square set on point.

Finished Quilt Size: 68½″ × 68½″ • **Finished Block Size:** 6″ × 6″

Materials

RAINBOW FABRICS

The colors are listed in the order in which they are used in paper piecing.

⅜ yard each of the following colors:

- Fabric 1: red
- Fabric 2: dark pink
- Fabric 3: orange
- Fabric 4: light pink
- Fabric 5: yellow
- Fabric 6: red-purple
- Fabric 7: light blue
- Fabric 8: green-blue
- Fabric 9: dark blue
- Fabric 10: green
- Fabric 11: purple
- Fabric 12: yellow-green

BACKGROUND FABRICS

- 3 yards of black polka dot
- 1⅔ yards of white polka dot

BACKING

- 4¼ yards

BINDING

- ⅔ yard of black polka dot

OTHER MATERIALS

- Paper for paper piecing the rainbow blocks
- 77″ × 77″ batting

Cut

PREPARE TEMPLATES

Prepare *Lucy in the Sky* Templates A and B from the patterns (pullout page P2). Make 25 copies each of Templates A and B for the rainbow squares. Trim each paper-piecing pattern about ½″ from outer border.

RAINBOW FABRICS

- From each rainbow color, cut 2 strips 6″ × fabric width. From each strip, cut 13 rectangles 2¾″ × 6″ (you need 25 rectangles total of each rainbow color).

BACKGROUND FABRICS

Black

- Cut 4 strips 6½″ × fabric width. From these strips, cut 24 squares 6½″ × 6½″.
- Cut 7 strips 7½″ × fabric width. From these strips, cut 32 squares 7½″ × 7½″.
- Cut 3 strips 7″ × fabric width. From these strips, cut 14 squares 7″ × 7″. Then cut each square on the diagonal (making 28 triangles).
- *Optional:* If you want the corners of the quilt to finish square, cut 2 squares 5″ × 5″ and cut in half diagonally to form 4 corner triangles (see Assemble, Step 4, page 37).

White

- From the white, cut 7 strips 7½″ × fabric width. From these strips, cut 32 squares 7½″ × 7½″.

PIECE

Paper-Pieced Rainbow Squares

1. Take a Template A and a rectangle 2¾˝ × 6˝ each of Fabrics 1 and 2. Match the 2 fabrics, right sides together. Align the wrong side of Fabric 1 to the unprinted side of the paper as indicated by Diagram 1. Make sure the fabric edges extend roughly ¼˝ beyond the line between areas 1 and 2. (Check by holding the pieces up to a lightbox or an overhead light.)

2. Pin the fabric in place on the paper. With the printed side of the paper up, sew along the line between areas 1 and 2, starting and ending ¼˝ beyond the line; I like to backstitch at the beginning and end of the seam for added strength.

3. Place the unit, fabric side down, on a cutting mat. Fold the paper along the just-sewn line to expose the seam allowance. Carefully trim the seam allowance to ¼˝ using the rotary cutter and ruler (Diagram 2).

Notes about Paper Piecing

- *Templates are always mirror images, which can get confusing. It helps to write the colors under each number or piece.*

- *Use a small stitch length when paper piecing. Follow the manufacturer's guidelines for your sewing machine to decrease stitch length to about 1.8 mm/stitch.*

- *A lightbox is handy when checking strip placement, but holding the template and strips up to a window or an overhead light works quite well too.*

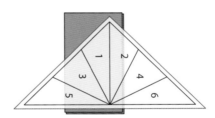

DIAGRAM 1

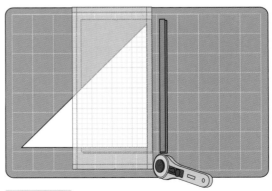

DIAGRAM 2

4. Unfold the unit and lay it, paper side down, on an ironing board. Press the seam to the side using a dry iron.

5. Align a 2¾″ × 6″ rectangle of Fabric 3 so that the edge of the fabric extends to roughly ¼″ past the line between pieces 1 and 3.

6. Pin in place. From the paper side, sew along the line between pieces 1 and 3 (Diagram 3).

7. Repeat Step 3 to carefully trim the seam allowance (Diagram 4). Press.

8. Repeat Steps 5–7 with Fabrics 4, 5, and 6 to complete the Template A unit.

9. After pressing and sewing Fabric 6, trim the excess fabric along the edges of the template. Be sure to leave a ¼″ seam allowance along all the edges, as indicated on the template.

10. Carefully remove the paper from the unit.

11. Repeat the process to make 25 Template A units and 25 Template B units.

12. Carefully pin and sew together the A and B units (Diagram 5). Press the center seam open.

13. If necessary, trim each rainbow block to 6½″ × 6½″. Make 25.

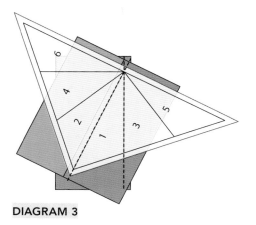

DIAGRAM 3

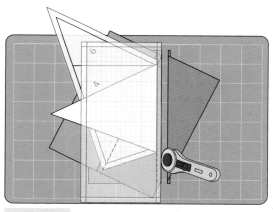

DIAGRAM 4

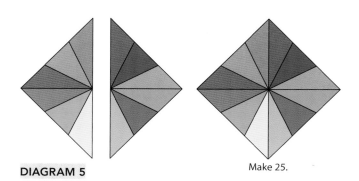

DIAGRAM 5

Make 25.

Hourglass Blocks

1. On the wrong side of the white 7½″ × 7½″ squares, draw a diagonal line with a fabric-marking pen.

2. Matching a black and a white square, right sides together, sew ¼″ from each side of the marked line (Diagram 6).

3. Lay the unit on a cutting mat and cut along the marked line. Without moving the unit, cut along the other diagonal to get 4 pieces (Diagram 7).

4. Press the seams toward the black.

5. Sew 2 pieces together, matching seams. Press the seams open. Each pair of 7½″ fabric squares makes 2 hourglass blocks (Diagram 8).

6. Repeat with the other pairs of black-and-white squares to make 64 hourglass blocks.

7. Trim the blocks to 6½″ × 6½″, keeping the X formed by the seams in the center of the block.

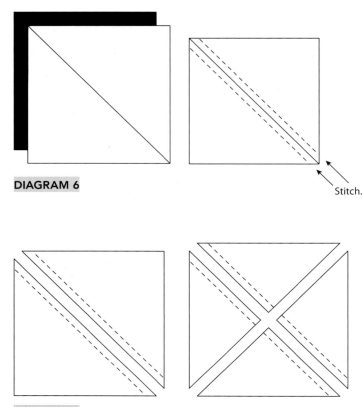

DIAGRAM 6

Stitch.

DIAGRAM 7

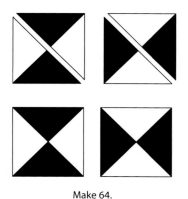

Make 64.

DIAGRAM 8

ASSEMBLE

1. Lay out the rainbow blocks, hourglass blocks, 6½″ × 6½″ black squares, and 7″ triangles in diagonal rows (Diagram 9).

TIP

Be sure the rainbow blocks are arranged the same way throughout the layout and as they are assembled into the quilt top.

2. Stitch the blocks into rows. Press the seams toward the hourglass blocks.

Note: The middle row (the one with seven rainbow blocks and eight hourglass blocks) does not have triangles at each end.

3. Piece the rows together. Press.

4. *Optional:* Sew the 4 corner triangles onto the corners of the quilt top. Press.

DIAGRAM 9

FINISH

Quilt

1. Make a quilt backing 76″ × 76″.

2. Baste the quilt sandwich using your favorite method (see Finishing the Quilt, page 25).

3. Quilt as desired.

4. Trim and square the quilt (see Squaring the Quilt, page 27).

Bind

Finish the binding as preferred (see Binding the Quilt, page 27).

DESIGN IDEAS

	Number of rainbow blocks	Number of hourglass blocks	Number of 6½″ × 6½″ squares	Number of triangles	Yardage
Baby quilt 36″ × 36″	5	16	4	12	¼ yard of each rainbow fabric 1¼ yards of black ½ yard of white
Crib quilt 51½″ × 51½″	13	36	12	20	¼ yard of each rainbow fabric 1¾ yards of black 1⅛ yards of white

BUBBLES

Inspired by the rainbow sheen reflecting off summertime bubbles, this happy quilt offers a new pattern for a classic block, the traditional Log Cabin, set on point.

As a kid, I always thought rainbows without purple were less than real rainbows. But now I can appreciate the absence of my favorite color, especially with reproduction fabrics.

I have always loved retro feed-sack fabrics. From the fabrics in my great-grandmothers' and grandmothers' quilts to the 1930s reproduction fabrics printed today, I love them all. Of course, they are especially great in color order.

Finished Quilt Size: 59¾″ × 79½″ • **Finished Block Size:** 19¾″ × 19¾″

Materials

BACKGROUND FABRICS
- 3 yards linen-cotton blend fabric

RAINBOW FABRICS
- ½ yard total of assorted reds
- ⅝ yard total of assorted oranges
- ⅝ yard total of assorted yellows
- ¾ yard total of assorted greens
- 1 yard total of assorted blues

BACKING
- 5 yards

BINDING
- ⅝ yard black

OTHER MATERIALS
- 68″ × 88″ batting

Cut

BACKGROUND FABRICS
- From linen, cut 2 strips 4½″ × fabric width. From strips, cut 12 squares 4½″ × 4½″.
- From linen, cut 8 strips 11″ × fabric width. Cut 3 squares 11″ × 11″ from each strip for a total of 24 linen squares. Then cut each square in half diagonally to get 48 triangles.

RAINBOW FABRICS
For each color, there is a "short," "medium," and "long" strip length.

- From red, cut 8 strips 1½″ × fabric width. Then from the strips, cut:
  - 12 strips 1½″ × 4½″
  - 24 strips 1½″ × 5½″
  - 12 strips 1½″ × 6½″

- From orange, cut 11 strips 1½″ × fabric width. Then from the strips, cut:
  - 12 strips 1½″ × 6½″
  - 24 strips 1½″ × 7½″
  - 12 strips 1½″ × 8½″

- From yellow, cut 13 strips 1½″ × fabric width. Then from the strips, cut:
  - 12 strips 1½″ × 8½″
  - 24 strips 1½″ × 9½″
  - 12 strips 1½″ × 10½″

- From green, cut 16 strips 1½″ × fabric width. Then from the strips, cut:
  - 12 strips 1½″ × 10½″
  - 24 strips 1½″ × 11½″
  - 12 strips 1½″ × 12½″

- From blue, cut 22 strips 1½″ × fabric width. Then from the strips, cut:
  - 12 strips 1½″ × 12½″
  - 24 strips 1½″ × 13½″
  - 12 strips 1½″ × 14½″

PIECE

Log Cabin Blocks

Note: Because of the narrowness of the Log Cabin pieces, press the seams to one side.

1. Sew a red 1½″ × 4½″ strip to the right-hand side of a linen 4½″ square. Press. Sew a red 1½″ × 5½″ strip to the top of the square. Press. Sew a red 1½″ × 5½″ strip to the left side of the square. Press. Finally, sew a red 1½″ × 6½″ strip to the bottom of the square. Press. Refer to Diagram 1. If necessary, square up the block to 6½″ × 6½″.

2. Sew an orange 1½″ × 6½″ strip to the right-hand side of the block. Press. Sew an orange 1½″ × 7½″ strip to the top of the block. Press. Sew an orange 1½″ × 7½″ strip to the left side of the block. Press. Sew an orange 1½″ × 8½″ strip to the bottom of the block. Press. Refer to Diagram 2. If necessary, square up the block to 8½″ × 8½″.

3. Following the process in Steps 1 and 2, sew yellow strips around the block, pressing after each strip is attached. Refer to Diagram 3. If necessary, square up the block to 10½″ × 10½″.

4. Following the process in Steps 1 and 2, sew green strips around the block, pressing after each strip is attached. Refer to Diagram 4. If necessary, square up the block to 12½″ × 12½″.

5. Following the process in Steps 1 and 2, sew blue strips around the block, pressing after each strip is attached. Refer to Diagram 5. If necessary, square up the block to 14½″ × 14½″.

6. Repeat Steps 1–5 to make the remaining 11 blocks.

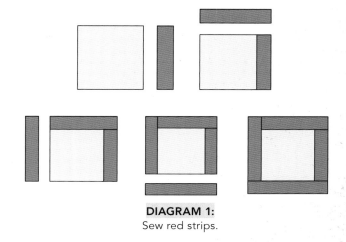

DIAGRAM 1:
Sew red strips.

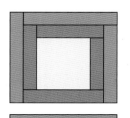

DIAGRAM 2:
Sew orange strips.

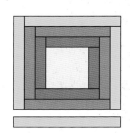

DIAGRAM 3:
Sew yellow strips.

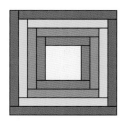

DIAGRAM 4:
Sew green strips.

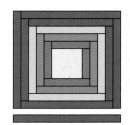

DIAGRAM 5:
Sew blue strips.

Setting Triangles

1. Sew 2 linen triangles to the upper left and lower right sides of the Log Cabin block. Press the seams open. Then sew 2 linen triangles to the upper right and lower left sides of the block and press the seams open (Diagram 6).

2. Repeat Step 1 on the remaining 11 Log Cabin blocks.

3. Trim and square all the blocks to 20¼″ × 20¼″.

ASSEMBLE

1. Sew the blocks together in rows, 3 to a row for 4 rows. Press the seams toward the middle block for the first and third rows. For the other 2 rows, press the seams toward the outer blocks.

2. Sew rows together. Press the seams as desired (Diagram 7).

DIAGRAM 6:
Sew corner triangles.

DIAGRAM 7:
Quilt assembly

FINISH

Quilt

1. Make a quilt backing to measure 68″ × 88″.

2. Baste the quilt sandwich using your favorite method (see Finishing the Quilt, page 25).

3. Quilt as desired. I quilted mine with straight lines using my walking foot. I didn't want perfection, so I casually echoed the previously quilted lines.

4. Trim and square the quilt (see Squaring the Quilt, page 27).

Bind

Finish the binding as preferred (see Binding the Quilt, page 27).

DESIGN IDEAS

Use the triangle background on each block to create a secondary pattern. Use one fabric for the triangles on the upper left and lower right. Use a second fabric for the triangles on the lower left and upper right.

To make a baby quilt, make 4 blocks and arrange them into 2 blocks × 2 blocks; to make a crib quilt, make 6 blocks and arrange them into 2 blocks × 3 blocks; to make a throw quilt, make 9 blocks and arrange them into 3 blocks × 3 blocks.

	Rainbow yardage	Background yardage	Number of blocks	Cut
Baby quilt 40″ × 40″	¼ yard reds ¼ yard oranges ¼ yard yellows ⅓ yard greens ⅜ yard blues	1¼ yards	Make 4 blocks.	Cut 4 short, 8 medium, and 4 long strips of each color, referring to the cutting instructions (page 40). Cut 4 linen squares 4½″. Cut 16 background triangles from 3 strips 11″ × fabric width.
Crib quilt 40″ × 59¾″	¼ yard reds ⅜ yard oranges ⅜ yard yellows ⅜ yard greens ½ yard blues	1½ yards	Make 6 blocks.	Cut 6 short, 12 medium, and 6 long strips of each color, referring to the cutting instructions (page 40). Cut 6 linen squares 4½″. Cut 24 background triangles from 4 strips 11″ × fabric width.
Throw quilt 59¾″ × 59¾″	⅓ yard reds ½ yard oranges ½ yard yellows ⅝ yard greens ¾ yard blues	2¼ yards	Make 9 blocks.	Cut 9 short, 18 medium, and 9 long strips of each color, referring to the cutting instructions (page 40). Cut 9 linen squares 4½″. Cut 36 background triangles from 6 strips 11″ × fabric width.

IRISH +

Simply pieced, this quilt is similar in construction to the classic Irish Chain pattern, but it also plays on the popular modern plus-sign quilts. The classic Irish Chain can be seen in the diagonal rows of white squares. The "pluses," alternating between high and low volume, carry the rainbow across the quilt.

Frequently, plus-sign quilts are pieced row by row. This fat quarter–friendly pattern uses a block and sash approach to piecing. For this quilt, I chose higher-volume rainbow fabrics for the rainbow pluses in the foreground and lower-volume rainbow fabrics for the rainbow pluses in the background.

Finished Quilt Size: 50½″ × 58½″ • Finished Block Size: 6″ × 6″

Materials

RAINBOW FABRICS

High-volume rainbow fabrics

- ¼ yard each of dark purple, dark blue, dark blue-green, dark lime green, dark yellow-orange, dark orange, and dark red

Low-volume rainbow fabrics

- ¼ yard each of light purple, light blue, light green, light yellow, light orange, and light red

BACKGROUND FABRIC

- 2⅛ yards white

BACKING

- 3¼ yards

BINDING

- ⅝ yard gray

OTHER MATERIALS

- 59″ × 67″ batting

Cut

RAINBOW FABRICS

High-volume fabrics

- From each high-volume rainbow fabric, cut 2 strips 2½″ × fabric width. From 1 strip, subcut 6 strips 2½″ × 6½″.

Low-volume fabrics

- From each low-volume rainbow fabric, cut 2 strips 2½″ × fabric width. From the first strip, subcut 5 strips 2½″ × 6½″. Cut the other strip in half to make 2 strips 2½″ × approximately 20″.

WHITE FABRIC

- Cut a strip 4½″ × fabric width. Cut this piece in half to make 2 pieces 4½″ × approximately 20″ for the A blocks.
- Cut 20 strips 2½″ × fabric width.
- Cut 3 strips 2½″ × fabric width. Subcut them in half to make 6 smaller strips 2½″ × 20″.
- Cut 3 strips 2½″ × fabric width. Subcut 24 squares 2½″ × 2½″ and 12 rectangles 2½″ × 4½″.

TIP If you are using fat quarters, just double the number of strips. For example, from the high-volume fabric, instead of 2 strips, cut 4 strips 2½″ × 20″.

PIECE

Note: Unless indicated, all seams are pressed toward the white.

A Blocks

In this step, we will piece the nine-patches that are along the top and bottom rows of the quilt top. These nine-patches are a bit different from the blocks in the center rows and different from your "usual" nine-patches. Let's call them A Blocks.

1. Piece together the 4½˝ × 20˝ white strip and a light purple 2½˝ × 20˝ strip. Press. From this strip set, subcut 5 strips 2½˝ × 6½˝ (Diagram 1).

2. Using 2 white strips 2½˝ × fabric width and a dark purple strip 2½˝ × fabric width, piece a strip set white / dark purple / white. Press. From this strip set, subcut 12 strips 2½˝ × 6½˝. Set 2 aside for quilt top assembly (Diagram 2).

3. Piece the units together as follows: white / dark purple / white, 4˝ white / light purple, white / dark purple / white. Press. Make 5 purple A Blocks (Diagram 3).

4. Repeat Steps 1–3 to make 5 red A Blocks (Diagram 4).

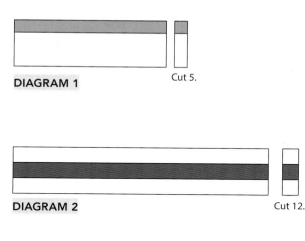

DIAGRAM 1   Cut 5.

DIAGRAM 2   Cut 12.

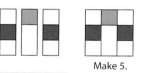

Make 5.

DIAGRAM 3:
Purple A blocks

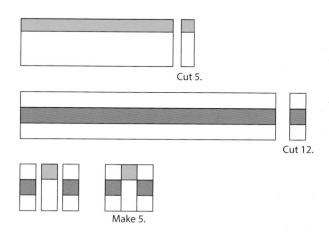

Cut 5.

Cut 12.

Make 5.

DIAGRAM 4: Red A Blocks

B Blocks

Now we will piece the Nine-Patch blocks in the center of the quilt top. Let's call these B Blocks. They are all the same, but the colors vary in each row. So pay attention to the orientation of the colors.

1. Piece the high-volume strip sets. Each strip set uses 1 high-volume fabric strip 2½″ × fabric width and 2 white strips 2½″ × fabric width. Press. Repeat for all high-volume fabrics (blue, blue-green, lime green, yellow-orange, orange).

From each strip set, subcut 12 strips 2½″ × 6½″. Set 2 strips aside for quilt top assembly (Diagram 5).

2. Piece each low-volume strip set using 2 low-volume fabric strips 2½″ × 20″ and 1 white strip 2½″ × 20″. First piece a strip set light purple/white/light blue. Press.

Repeat this step for the following groupings (refer to Diagram 6):

- light blue/white/light green
- light green/white/light yellow
- light yellow/white/light orange
- light orange/white/light red

From each strip set, subcut 5 strips 2½″ × 6½″ (Diagram 6).

3. Piece the B Blocks. Take 2 white/dark blue/white strips and a light purple/white/light blue strip and piece them together into a nine-patch. Press the seams open. Make 5 (Diagram 7).

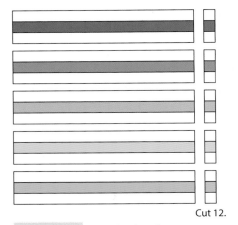

Cut 12.

DIAGRAM 5: Piece high-volume strip sets.

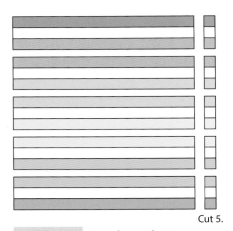

Cut 5.

DIAGRAM 6: Piece low-volume strip sets.

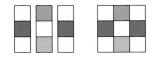

DIAGRAM 7: Piece B Blocks.

Repeat Step 3 with the following groupings:

- 2 white / dark blue-green / white, and a light blue / white / light green

- 2 white / dark green / white, and a light green / white / light yellow

- 2 white / dark orange-yellow / white, and a light yellow / white / light orange

- 2 white / dark orange / white, and a light orange / white / light red (Diagram 8)

ASSEMBLE

On a design wall, lay out the quilt blocks row by row in order, starting with the purple A blocks at the top. Place the appropriate high-volume 2½" × 6½" strip and a white / high-volume / white unit from Step 2 of A Blocks (page 47) to each end of each row. Refer to the quilt assembly diagram (Diagram 9).

1. Piece the blocks together horizontally and by color. Press.

2. Piece the horizontal, low-volume sashing together. Sew the low-volume 2½" × 6½" rectangles to the 2½" white squares. On either end sew a 2½" × 4½" white rectangle. Press. Refer to Diagram 9.

3. Sew the rows together, row by row. Press.

4. Finally, sew the 6 strips of white 2½" × fabric width together end to end. Press the seams open. From this length of strips, cut 2 lengths 46½" and 2 lengths 58½". Sew the 2 shorter strips to the top and bottom of the quilt top. Press. Trim if necessary. Sew the 2 longer strips to each side. Press.

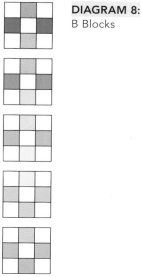

DIAGRAM 8:
B Blocks

Make 5 of each.

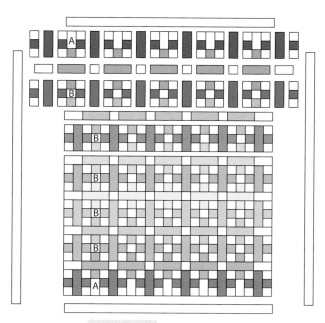

DIAGRAM 9: Quilt assembly

FINISH

Quilt

1. Make a quilt backing 59″ × 67″.

2. Baste the quilt sandwich using your favorite method (see Finishing the Quilt, page 25).

3. Quilt as desired. I hand quilted mine using a simple crosshatch along the white Irish Chain for a perfect, cuddly finish.

4. Trim and square the quilt (see Squaring the Quilt, page 27).

Bind

Finish the binding as preferred (see Binding the Quilt, page 27).

DESIGN IDEAS

This quilt would look fantastic in a more limited palette. How about gray for the pluses in the foreground and mustard for the pluses in the background? Or maybe blue and red? Oh dear, I feel another quilt coming on!

RAINBOW STREAK

To my surprise, the popular Chevron quilt—also known as a Zigzag or Streak of Lightning quilt—is not an invention of modern quilting. The Streak of Lightning quilt pattern is an old favorite, dating back to the days of the pioneers. The lasting appeal of the pattern no doubt finds its roots in the repeating visuals, versatility, and adaptability. Zigzag quilts can be constructed from half-square triangle blocks or using a more intricate block such as the Log Cabin.

My version, *Rainbow Streak*, uses fabric sewn together in strip sets and then cut at 60° angles. If you are familiar with piecing a traditional Lone Star quilt, you may find the construction similar. The cut strips are pieced together with background parallelograms. While the piecing is relatively easy, pieces are sewn on the bias, which adds a bit of difficulty. Pay close attention to the orientation of the color order, because the direction of the zigzag changes back and forth between color groupings.

Finished Quilt Size: 61½″ × 72½″

Materials

RAINBOW FABRICS INCLUDING BINDING
A total of 36 fabrics are required: 6 each of purple, blue, green, yellow, orange, and pink. For the first and last colors of the rainbow (Fabrics 1 and 36), a ¼-yard cut of fabric is needed. For the other 34 colors you'll need 1 strip 2½″ × fabric width, or ⅛ yard.

BACKGROUND FABRIC
- 5¼ yards solid

BACKING
- 4 yards

OTHER MATERIALS
- 70″ × 81″ batting

A Note on Fabric Selection

To create a seamless, low-contrast transition across the rainbow, choose fabrics that are subtly different from one another. Each should play a role in moving from the previous adjacent color to the next adjacent color. For a higher-contrast rainbow, choose six similarly hued colors within each color group (for example, six red-purples, six China blues, and so on).

Cut

RAINBOW FABRICS

- From each of the 36 colors, cut 1 strip 2½″ × fabric width. Sort the strips into 6 color groups: purple, blue, green, yellow, orange, and pink. Cut 2 additional strips 2½″ × fabric width from each of Fabric 1 (darkest purple) and Fabric 36 (lightest pink), and set aside for the binding.

BACKGROUND FABRIC

- To cut the background parallelograms, first cut 9 strips 19″ × fabric width from the solid background yardage. Keep the fabric folded as it was on the bolt, and trim off the selvages. Working from the top (where the selvage was) cut 2 sets of 2 parallelograms (Diagram 1A). Refer to Cutting at an Angle (page 19). Open up the fabric at the fold, reposition the fabric, and cut an additional parallelogram with the same angles. You'll have a total of 5 parallelograms.

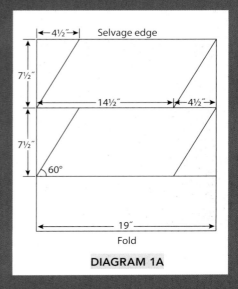

DIAGRAM 1A

The parallelograms should measure 14½″ on the longest side and 7½″ wide. Repeat the process to cut 20 parallelograms from Diagram 1A.

If you're cutting the fabric with wrong sides together, the parallelograms on the bottom layer will have a 120° angle in the left and upper right corners—in other words, they'll be opposite to the ones in the top layer. So one 19″ piece of fabric will yield 3 parallelograms 60° and 2 parallelograms 120°.

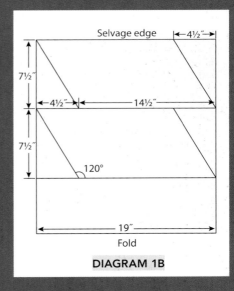

DIAGRAM 1B

Cut an additional 20 parallelograms at a 120° angle, or by flipping the direction of the parallelogram (Diagram 1B). From your last piece of background fabric, still folded, cut one more pair of parallelograms—this will give you a total of 42 parallelograms with 21 of each type.

If you're using solid fabrics, you don't need to flip the angle of the parallelograms when you cut the second set—just flip the pieces over after you've cut them.

PIECE THE ROWS

1. Beginning with the purple group of strips, sew the 6 strips together in rainbow color order. Press the seams toward the pink end of the rainbow. Repeat with the remaining 5 color groups until you have 6 sets, a set in each color.

2. From each of the 6 color sets, cut 2 strips 2½″ wide and set aside; these will be used to make the binding.

3. Next, group the color sets into the following groups:

   Group 1: purple, green, and orange

   Group 2: blue, yellow, and pink

4. From Group 1, cut 6 strips 2½″ wide at a 60° angle (see Cutting Angled Units, page 20).

5. From Group 2, cut 6 strips 2½″ wide at a 120° angle (see Diagram 2). *Be sure to maintain the same rainbow order across groups while cutting.*

Cut a total of 36 diagonal strips, 6 from each color.

6. Working with strips from Group 1, piece the color strips to the background parallelograms. Press the seam toward the background.

7. Piece the color strips from Group 2 to the background parallelograms. Press the seam toward the color as indicated by the arrows in Diagram 3.

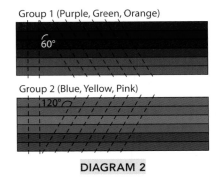

Group 1 (Purple, Green, Orange)

60°

Group 2 (Blue, Yellow, Pink)

120°

DIAGRAM 2

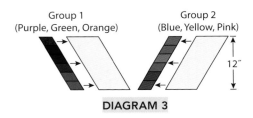

Group 1
(Purple, Green, Orange)

Group 2
(Blue, Yellow, Pink)

12″

DIAGRAM 3

TIP

The blocks in this pattern are irregularly shaped, so be sure to align the match points (see Match Points, page 22).

ASSEMBLE

1. Piece the blocks together into rows, working by color groupings. Be sure to sew an additional background parallelogram to the remaining color strip. Refer to Diagram 4. For Group 1 rows, press the seams toward the background. For Group 2 rows, press the seams toward the colors.

2. Piece the rows together in pairs (purple and blue, green and yellow, and orange and pink), being sure to match the zigzags between rows (see Diagram 5). Press the seams toward the pink end of the rainbow.

3. Sew pairs of rows together. Press the seams as shown (Diagram 6).

4. Trim the angled edges from the quilt top and square up the quilt to measure 61½″ × 72½″. Alternatively, this step may be completed after quilting.

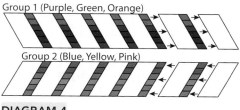

Group 1 (Purple, Green, Orange)

Group 2 (Blue, Yellow, Pink)

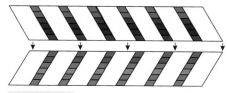

DIAGRAM 4

DIAGRAM 5

DIAGRAM 6

FINISH

Quilt

1. Make a quilt backing 70″ × 81″.

2. Baste the quilt sandwich using your favorite method (see Finishing the Quilt, page 25).

3. Quilt as desired. I quilted mine using straight-line quilting to create the illusion of zigzags in the background.

4. Trim and square the quilt (see Squaring the Quilt, page 27).

Bind

1. Using the 2½″ × 2½″ color group sets from Piece the Rows, Step 2 (page 54), make a binding set by sewing together a 2½″ × fabric-width strip of Fabric 1, a purple strip, a blue strip, a green strip, a yellow strip, an orange strip, a pink strip, and a 2½″ × fabric-width strip of Fabric 36 (see Preparing a Continuous Binding Strip, page 27). Be sure to sew the strips together in color order. Press the seams toward the pink end of the rainbow. Repeat to make a second binding strip.

2. Attach each binding set separately by first matching the rainbow binding to the rainbow in the quilt (see image below). Secure with clips or pins.

Align rainbow in binding to rainbow in quilt.

3. After sewing the binding sets to the quilt, join the purple Fabric 1 strips at the midpoint of the top edge and the Fabric 36 strips at the midpoint of the bottom edge. Finish the binding as preferred (see Binding the Quilt, page 27).

DESIGN IDEA

Baby Quilt Size: 43½″ × 48½″

Fabric	Yardage	Cutting	Piecing
Rainbow fabric	24 total colors are needed to make 4 color groupings (6 fabrics each).	Cut 24 strips 2½″ × fabric width.	Piece 4 groups of color strip sets. Cut 4 strips 2½″ wide from each of the 4 color sets.
Background fabric	2½ yards	Cut 10 parallelograms at a 60° angle. Cut 10 parallelograms at a 120° angle.	
Backing	3 yards		Piece a backing 52″ × 57″.
Binding	An additional 2 strips 2½″ × fabric width each from Fabric 1 and Fabric 24	Cut 2 strips 2½″ × fabric width from each of the 4 color sets and 2 additional strips 2½″ × fabric width each from Fabric 1 and Fabric 24.	
Batting	52″ × 57″		

SCATTERED

This easy, low-volume patchwork quilt boasts a quiet rainbow. My favorite low-volume fabrics fill the background. This quilt goes together quickly and easily, making it a fun beginner quilt. The instructions for replicating this quilt are as follows, but don't be afraid to change up the layout of the rainbow charms.

Finished Quilt Size: 54½″ × 68″

Materials

QUILT TOP FABRICS

- A total of 3 yards assorted low-volume fabrics
- 40 rainbow-colored charm squares 5″ × 5″ (or 1 charm pack)

BACKING FABRICS

- 3½ yards backing fabric

BINDING FABRICS

- ⅝ yard binding fabric

OTHER MATERIALS

- 63″ × 76″ batting

A Note about Fabric Selection

To make the rainbow charms pop, I chose to confine my low-volume fabric selections to my favorite black-on-white and black-on-cream combinations. I still ended up using more than ten different fabrics!

Cut

BACKGROUND FABRICS

In addition to the 40 rainbow charm squares, which are 5″ squares, you will need 140 low-volume charm squares. Cut a total of 18 strips 5″ × fabric width. From each strip, cut 8 charm squares, 5″ × 5″. (You will have 4 extra squares.)

PIECE

You have some options before beginning. You can either lay out the rainbow charm squares to match the quilt assembly diagram (page 60) until you're satisfied, or you can randomly piece the charms together.

1. Piece the charm squares together into units of 2 charms (Diagram 1).

2. Piece the units of 2 charm squares together into units of 4 charms (Diagram 1).

3. Piece by row: Piece 3 units of 4 charm squares into a row. Make 15 rows. Press the seams in alternating directions (Diagram 2).

TIP

How do you randomize your piecing? I know of three different ways to be "random":

- Some of my friends throw all the fabrics into a brown paper bag and just pull squares out. Whatever comes out, they use.

- Some prefer a bit more control and lay out the pieces in sorted piles. Then they select each piece of fabric from a pile.

- Still other friends aren't so random, and they piece fabrics that match so that pairs of squares or grouping have some order throughout the quilt.

Can you guess which method I used?

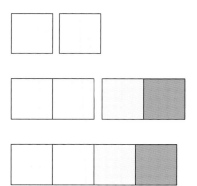

DIAGRAM 1: Piece charm squares into units.

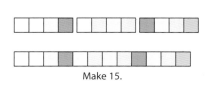

Make 15.

DIAGRAM 2: Piece into rows.

ASSEMBLE

1. Assemble the quilt top by sewing the 15 rows together. Press (Diagram 3).

2. Sew rows together. Press.

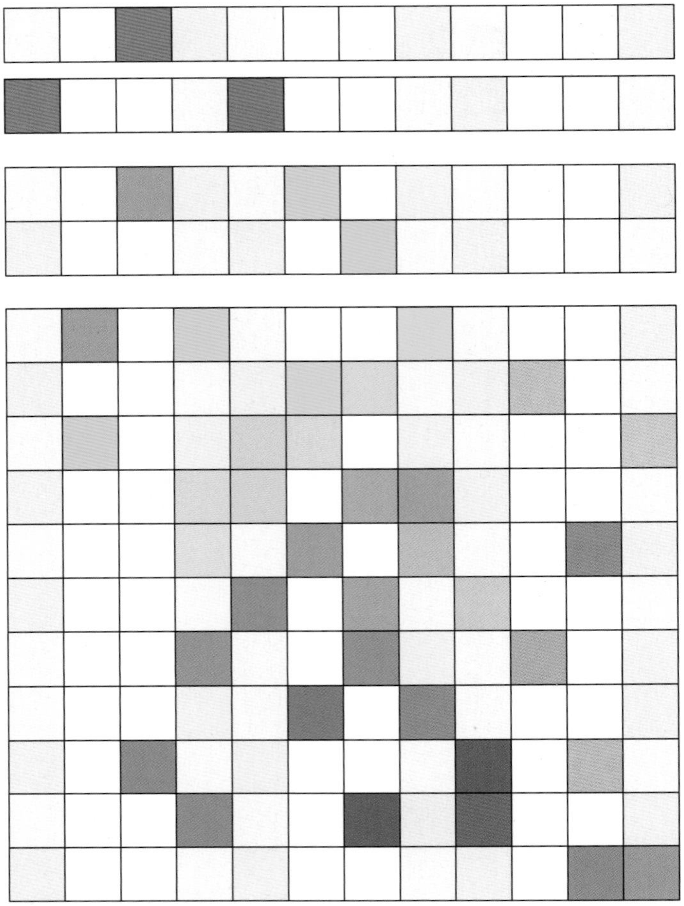

FINISH

Quilt

1. Make a quilt backing 63″ × 76″.

2. Baste the quilt sandwich using your favorite method (see Finishing the Quilt, page 25).

3. Quilt as desired.

4. Trim and square the quilt (see Squaring the Quilt, page 27).

Bind

Finish the binding as preferred (see Binding the Quilt, page 27).

DIAGRAM 3: Quilt assembly

DESIGN IDEA

You can easily make a baby quilt from this design, measuring 41″ × 45½″. You will need 90 charm squares laid out in 10 rows of 9 squares each. Remember that you can cut 56 charm squares from a yard of fabric.

MODERN QUILTS

Quilts in this section are inspired by modern design.

Some use negative space as a design element. In *Huckleberry* and *In the Throne Room*, I used the negative space to explore how quilting accentuates the design.

Some quilts within this section, *Huckleberry* and *Ducks in a Row*, use repetition of a single shape as a design.

HUCKLEBERRY

Every sewing room needs a color wheel. Scratch that. Every sewing room needs a *handmade* color wheel. This wallhanging-sized quilt beautifully captures the color wheel using simple, repeating shapes. It looks hard, but making it is rather straightforward and manageable. Hexagons are pieced into diamonds, and groups of four are then pieced into the larger diamond block.

The hexagons in the center ring are of darker values; the middle ring, of medium values; the outer ring, of lighter values. The background can be enlarged to make the quilt into a throw- or bed-sized quilt.

Finished Quilt Size: 40½″ × 40½″ • **Finished Block Size:** Approximately 5″ × 7″

Materials

RAINBOW FABRICS

TIP The first challenge is choosing the fabrics because 72 different colors are needed. I started by choosing my inner ring of fabrics, which are the darker values. Once I had those, I moved on to choosing the fabrics for the middle ring. And then, finally, I chose the ones for the outer ring.

- 24 high-value rainbow fabrics: 1 square 2¾″ × 2¾″ of each
- 24 medium-value rainbow fabrics: 2 squares 2¾″ × 2¾″ of each
- 24 low value-rainbow fabrics: 1 square 2¾″ × 2¾″ of each

BACKGROUND FABRICS
Yardage requirements for this pattern assume 41″ usable fabric width.

- 2¾ yards gray

BACKING
- 2¾ yards

BINDING
- ½ yard

OTHER MATERIALS
- 49″ × 49 ″ square of batting
- Template plastic or thin cardboard

Cut

PREPARE TEMPLATES
Prepare Templates A and B, and Trimming Template C from the patterns (pullout page P1).

TIP Making sure your templates are as accurate as possible will aid in the piecing of the diamonds later. Hint: Be sure the hexagon is symmetrical around its center!

Cut continued

RAINBOW FABRICS

From each 2¾″ square, cut a hexagon using Template A, as follows: 2 hexagons from each medium-value fabric and 1 each from the high-value and low-value fabrics. Cut a total of 96 hexagons.

BACKGROUND FABRICS

From gray

- Cut 6 strips 1⅜″ × fabric width. From each strip, cut 32 triangles using Template B. You will need a total of 192 triangles (see Using the Templates to Cut Pattern Pieces, page 21).

- Cut 8 strips of fabric 5″ × fabric width. From each strip, cut 12 rectangles 3″ × 5″ for a total of 96 rectangles.

- Cut 2 strips of fabric 20½″ × fabric width. Cut 2 squares 20½″ × 20½″ from each strip. Mark the fabric as shown in Diagram 1. To do so, tie a string to a fabric-marking pen. Hold the end of the string at the corner, and mark the 12½″ quarter-circle with the pen. Make sure the string is taut and not loose. Then mark the 19″ quarter-circle. Cut carefully along each of the marked lines and set these pieces aside. Repeat with the other 20½″ squares.

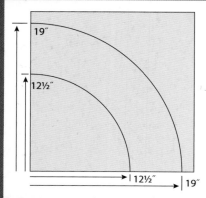

DIAGRAM 1: Mark background quarter-circles.

PIECE

1. Sew 2 B triangles to an A hexagon to make a small diamond unit (Diagram 2). Press the seams open. Repeat to make 96 small diamond units.

2. Piece 4 small diamond units into a large diamond unit (Diagram 3). Make 24 large diamond units.

3. Sew large diamond units into blocks. Sew 2 rectangles 3″ × 5″ to the lower right and upper left sides. Press the seams toward rectangles. Then sew 2 rectangles to the upper right and lower left sides. Press (Diagram 4).

4. Trim using Trimming Template C. *Make sure the darker-value hexagon is toward the smaller end of the trimming template.* Line up the horizontal line on the template with the center points of the middle hexagons (refer to Diagram 5). Trace Template C with a fabric-marking pen. Trim using a rotary cutter and ruler on the straight edges and with scissors on the curved edges.

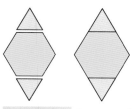

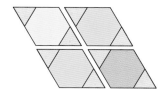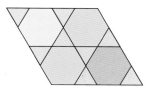

DIAGRAM 2: Piece small diamond units.

DIAGRAM 3: Piece large diamond unit.

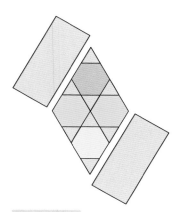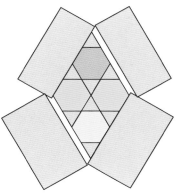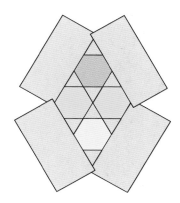

DIAGRAM 4: Sew diamonds into blocks.

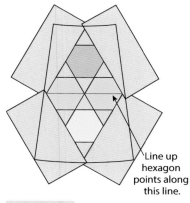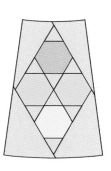

Line up hexagon points along this line.

DIAGRAM 5: Trim blocks.

TIPS

Regardless of the trimming template, it is important that the hexagons at the side have a ¼˝ seam allowance. If the hexagons at the sides fall outside the seamline on the template, add the ¼˝ seam allowance using a ruler, keeping it parallel to the sides of the trimming template.

The blocks were designed so that when the diamond blocks are pieced together, the diamond points will align. Because of this design, the diamonds will lean a bit.

ASSEMBLE

1. Lay out blocks in color order to form the circle. Working in 4 groups of 6 blocks, sew 6 blocks into a quarter-circle. Be sure to match the points where the diamonds intersect. Press the seams open. Sew 4 quarter-circles (Diagram 6).

2. Sew each quarter-circle to the inner and outer background pieces to make quarter units (Diagram 7). Press the seams toward the background. Refer to Sewing Curves (page 22).

3. Sew the quarter units into half units. Sew 2 quarters together. Make sure to match where the diamonds and the circles intersect. Press the seams to 1 side. Sew the remaining 2 quarters together and press the seams to the opposite side.

4. Piece the half units together, matching the rings, the diamond intersections, and the center seams (Diagram 8). Press.

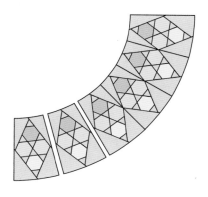

DIAGRAM 6: Sew blocks into quarter-circles.

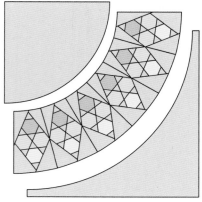

DIAGRAM 7: Piece quarter-circles to inner and outer backgrounds.

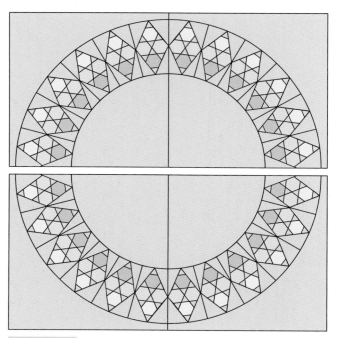

DIAGRAM 8: Quilt assembly

FINISH

Quilt

1. Make a quilt backing 49˝ × 49˝.

2. Baste the quilt sandwich using your favorite method (see Finishing the Quilt, page 25).

3. Quilt as desired.

4. Square the quilt (see Squaring the Quilt, page 27).

Bind

Finish the binding as preferred (see Binding the Quilt, page 27).

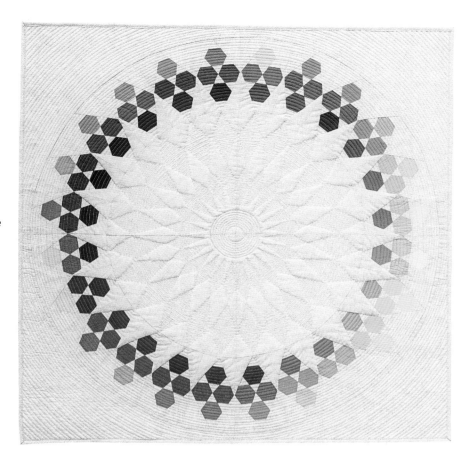

DESIGN IDEAS

This quilt would work well with your favorite charm pack—or candy packs—plus background yardage. Or pay homage to your favorite scraps.

To make this quilt larger, simply cut the background quarter-circles from larger pieces of the background fabric. Draw and cut 12½˝ and 19˝ quarter-circles (Diagram 9) from the inner corner of each rectangle as shown.

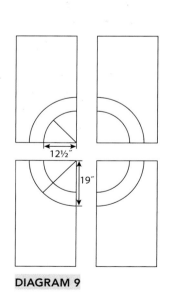

DIAGRAM 9

	Total background yardage needed	Cut 4 rectangles...
Throw quilt 66˝ × 76˝	5⅓ yards	33¼˝ × 38¼˝
Twin quilt 66˝ × 88˝	6½ yards	33¼˝ × 44¼˝
Full quilt 80˝ × 88˝	6½ yards	40¼˝ × 44¼˝

FLAME

Inspired by the flame of a candle, pieced diamonds are the main focus of this quilt. Variances in value lend an element of unpredictability to the predictable rainbow while also adding depth and dimension. Low-value diamond blocks paint the background, adding further visual interest. You can also choose to make this quilt in a "non-scrappy" version by using the same three fabrics in each diamond.

Finished Quilt Size: 69½″ × 68″ • **Finished Block Size:** 7″ × 12″

Materials

FLAME FABRICS

Scrappy version:

- ¾ yard assorted scraps for inner diamonds—each at least 2½″ × 5″ (A)
- 1¾ yards assorted scraps for first layer (B and C)
- 2¾ yards assorted scraps for second layer (D and E)

Non-scrappy version:

- ⅝ yard for inner diamonds (A)
- 1⅛ yards for first layer (B and C)
- 2 yards for second layer (D and E)

TIP To cut the fabric for the flames, you can follow the directions for either scrappy cutting or non-scrappy cutting.

SASHING

- 2⅞ yards

BACKING

- 4¼ yards

BINDING

- ⅝ yard

Flame block

OTHER MATERIALS

- 78″ × 76″ batting

Cut

TIP Make sure to cut all of the angled pieces for this project right side up so that the angles will go in the right direction!

RAINBOW FABRICS

Scrappy cutting

To cut scrappy flames, cut fabric for a single flame unit or a few at a time. You will need 72 flames. I chose to cut 44 rainbow flames (2 red-purple, 2 purple, 6 blue, 4 blue-green, 5 green, 5 green-yellow, 4 yellow, 5 gold, 5 orange, 3 red-orange, 2 pink, and 1 magenta).

I cut the remaining 28 flames from various neutrals.

To cut for 1 flame:

1. Cut a diamond. From scraps, cut a strip of fabric 2½″ × 5″. Cut a 60° angle at an end. Then make a second 60° cut 2½″ from the first cut (see Cutting Diamonds, page 20).

Cut continued

2. Cut the first layer. From a second scrap, cut a strip of fabric 2½˝ × 11˝. Cut a 60° diamond 2½˝ wide for Piece B and a 120° strip 4½˝ wide (see Cutting Angled Units, page 20).

3. Cut the second layer. From a third scrap, cut a strip of fabric 2½˝ × 18˝. Cut a 60° strip 4½˝ wide for Piece D and a 120° strip 6½˝ wide for Piece E (Diagram 1).

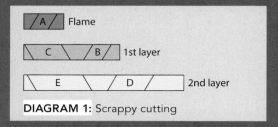

DIAGRAM 1: Scrappy cutting

Non-scrappy cutting

- From yardage for diamonds, cut 6 strips 2½˝ × fabric width. From each strip, cut 15 diamonds 2½˝ at 60°. This makes a total of 72 diamonds.

- From the yardage for the first layer, cut 17 strips 2½˝ × fabric width. From 6 strips, subcut 72 diamonds 2½˝ at 60°. From 11 strips, subcut 72 strips 4½˝ at 120° (see Cutting Angled Units, page 20).

- From the yardage for the second layer, cut 26 strips 2½˝ × fabric width. Then from 15 strips, subcut 72 strips 6½˝ at 120°. From 11 strips, subcut 72 strips 4½˝ at 60°.

TIP To cut angled units, especially 6½˝ sashing strips, you will need to unfold the fabric.

SASHING

- Cut 17 strips 2½˝ × fabric width. From each strip, subcut 5 strips 6½˝ at 60°, for a total of 84 strips.
- Cut 22 strips 2½˝ × fabric width.

PIECE

Press all seams open.

1. Sew the first-layer diamond (B) to the top of the inner diamond (A). Refer to Match Points (page 22). Press.

2. Sew the first-layer 4½˝ strip (C) to the right of the 2-diamond unit. Press.

3. Sew the second-layer 4½˝ strip (D) to the top of the diamond unit. Press.

4. Sew the second-layer 6½˝ strip (E) to the right of the unit. Press (Diagram 2).

Make 72 flame blocks.

DIAGRAM 2: Flame block assembly

ASSEMBLE

Press all seams open.

1. To the right-hand side of each block, sew a 6½˝ sashing strip as shown. Press (Diagram 3).

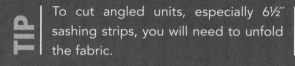

DIAGRAM 3: Attach sashing.

2. Sew the blocks together into rows by

DIAGRAM 4: Sew blocks into rows.

color (Diagram 4). Make 4 rows with 9 blocks each and 1 row each of 8 blocks, 7 blocks, 6 blocks, 5 blocks, 4 blocks, 3 blocks, 2 blocks, and 1 block (see quilt assembly diagram, page 73). There should be a 6½˝ sashing strip between each block. On each row sew an additional 6½˝ sashing strip to the block on the left. Press.

3. Sew a 2½″ × fabric width sashing strip to the

DIAGRAM 5: Sash tops

top of each row. Leave approximately 3″ on either side of the blocks at the ends. For some rows, 2 or 3 strips will need to be sewn together to make the sashing long enough. Press (Diagram 5).

4. Sew the rows together in color order. Press (Diagram 6).

5. Trim and square up the quilt top, leaving a ¼″ seam allowance on all sides.

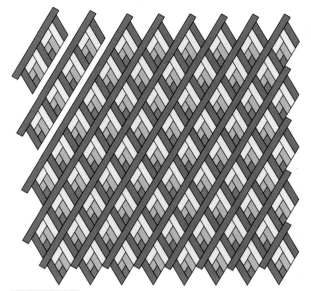

DIAGRAM 6: Quilt assembly

FINISH

Quilt

1. Make a quilt backing 76″ × 78″.

2. Baste the quilt sandwich using your favorite method (see Finishing the Quilt, page 25).

3. Quilt as desired.

4. Trim the backing and batting to the same size as the quilt top. Square the quilt (see Squaring the Quilt, page 27).

Bind

Finish the binding as preferred (see Binding the Quilt, page 27).

DESIGN IDEA

Change up the look by giving the quilt the illusion of a border. For each row, replace the flame blocks on either end with 6½″ diamonds cut from the background fabric.

IN THE THRONE ROOM

In the Book of Revelation, the last book of the Bible, the author, John, speaks of seeing the throne room of God, "and there was a rainbow around the throne, like an emerald in appearance" (Revelation 4:3). This quilt is my vision of this verse. The rainbow pattern is repeated throughout the quilt—front, back, and binding—capturing the infinite. To depict a gleam, the quilt also features both machine quilting and rainbow-colored hand quilting in concentric circles starting from the upper left quadrant.

Finished Quilt Size: 44½˝ × 50½˝ • **Finished Block Size:** 2˝ × 12˝

Materials

RAINBOW FABRIC (for quilt front and back)

■ ⅛ yard each of 24 different-colored solids

I chose to keep the contrast between the fabrics fairly low, with a few surprises. The fabrics that are higher in contrast provide the viewer's eye a hint that the rainbow is made out of more than one fabric.

BACKGROUND FABRIC (for quilt front and back)

■ 3¼ yards background fabric

BINDING

■ ½ yard

OTHER MATERIALS

■ 53˝ × 58˝ batting

■ Perle threads in a rainbow of colors

Note: Because this quilt repeats the quilt top on the backing, the pattern instructs you to make both the front and the backing at the same time.

Cut

RAINBOW FABRIC

■ From each of the 24 rainbow solids, cut 2 strips, 1˝ × fabric width.

BACKGROUND FABRIC

■ Refer to Diagram 1. From the background fabric, cut 2 pieces *on the fold* 13¼˝ × 50½˝ and 2 pieces *on the fold* 2½˝ × 6¼˝. Cut 1 pair of rectangles 6½˝ × 50½˝, and cut 13 pairs of rectangles 2½˝ × 12½˝ (one pair will be cut on the fold).

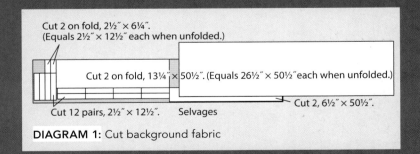

Cut 2 on fold, 2½˝ × 6¼˝.
(Equals 2½˝ × 12½˝ each when unfolded.)

Cut 2 on fold, 13¼˝ × 50½˝. (Equals 26½˝ × 50½˝ each when unfolded.)

Cut 12 pairs, 2½˝ × 12½˝.   Selvages   Cut 2, 6½˝ × 50½˝.

DIAGRAM 1: Cut background fabric

PIECE

1. Piece 2 rainbow strip sets by piecing a strip of each color together in color order. Each strip set should have 24 fabrics. Because these strips are small, press the seams to the side (Diagram 2).

2. From each strip set, cut 13 rainbow units 2½″ × 12½″. Set 2 rainbow units aside for the binding (Diagram 3).

3. Sew 12 rainbow units to 13 background strips 2½″ × 12½″ to make the center rainbow unit. Press the seams open. Make 2 center rainbow units (Diagram 4).

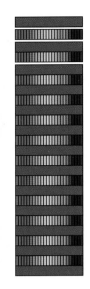

Make 2 strip sets.   Cut 13 from each strip set.

DIAGRAM 2: Piece rainbow strip sets.

DIAGRAM 3: Cut 13 rainbow units from strip sets.

DIAGRAM 4: Piece center rainbow units.

ASSEMBLE

1. Piece the quilt top by sewing the center rainbow unit to the left (26½″ × 50½″) and right (6½″ × 50½″) background pieces. The larger background piece should be on the red side of the center rainbow unit. Press toward background (Diagram 5).

2. Piece the quilt backing in the same fashion.

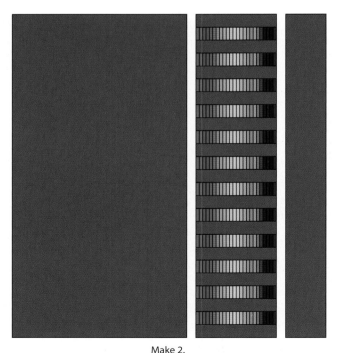

Make 2.

DIAGRAM 5: Quilt assembly

FINISH

Quilt

1. Make a quilt sandwich by layering the quilt back (right side down), batting, and quilt top (right side up). *During the quilt sandwich–making process, be sure first to line up the center rainbow units. Then match the corners of the quilt top and backing.* Baste the quilt sandwich well using your favorite method (see Finishing the Quilt, page 25).

2. Quilt as desired. I quilted concentric circles starting in the upper left quadrant of the quilt top. I marked the first circle using a regular drinking glass, but the rest were quilted freehand for an organic, imperfect look. I alternated hand quilting with rainbow-colored perle threads and machine quilting in white (Diagram 6).

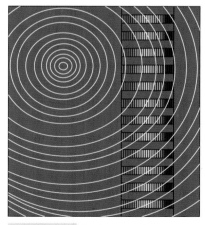

DIAGRAM 6: Quilting circles

3. Trim the backing and batting to the same size as the quilt top. Square up the quilt (see Squaring the Quilt, page 27).

Bind

1. Make a binding set by sewing together a background strip, a rainbow unit, and 2 background strips end to end. Press (see Preparing a Continuous Binding Strip, page 27). Repeat to make a second strip the same way.

2. Attach each binding separately by first aligning the rainbow binding with the rainbow in the quilt.

3. Finish the binding as preferred (see Binding the Quilt, page 27).

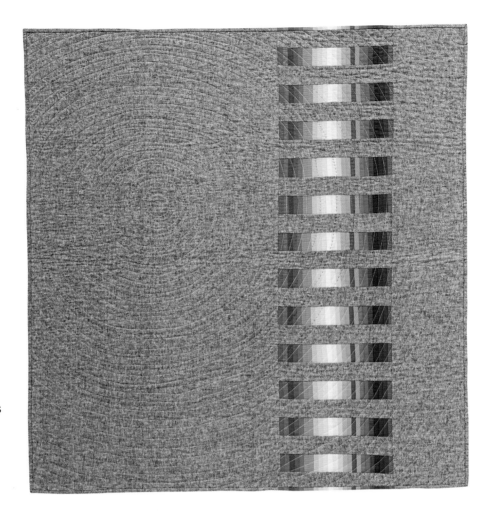

DESIGN IDEA

Instead of 24 strips of color, you may choose 12 colors. Instead of cutting 1″ strips from each fabric, cut 1½″ strips.

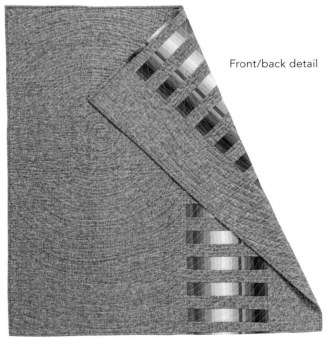

Front/back detail

DUCKS
IN A ROW

Quilted by Angela Walters

For this quilt, I wanted to show a spectrum palette that wasn't necessarily a full rainbow, so I chose to leave off the true reds, true blues, and purples. This quilt would look fantastic in all rainbow fabrics, though.

The "ducks" and background pieces are cut from templates. Once the cutting is done, the sewing is fairly simple.

Finished Quilt Size: 71½″ × 93½″

Materials

RAINBOW FABRICS

I used 4 or 5 fabrics in each color to reach these total amounts:

- ⅔ yard red-oranges
- ⅔ yard oranges
- ⅔ yard yellows
- ⅔ yard limes
- ⅔ yard light greens
- ⅔ yard teals
- ⅔ yard blue-greens

BACKGROUND FABRICS

I used 8–10 different fabrics for the background.

- 5½ yards (total)

BACKING

- 5⅔ yards

BINDING

- ¾ yard

OTHER MATERIALS

- 80″ × 102″ batting

Cut

PREPARE TEMPLATES

Prepare duck templates from the patterns: Short A, Tall A, Short B, Tall B, Short C, Tall C, Short D, and Tall D. Also prepare the background templates from the patterns: Short A, Tall A, Short B, Tall B, Short C, Tall C, Short D, and Tall D (pullout pages P1 and P2).

RAINBOW FABRICS

From each of 7 colors, cut 3 of each duck template, for a total of 21 ducks of each size.

	First cut	Second cut
Template Duck A	From a strip of fabric 4¼″ × fabric width, use template Tall Duck A to cut 3 *Tall* Duck A triangles.	Trim the strip's width to 3¼″. Using template Short Duck A, cut 3 *Short* Duck A triangles.
Template Duck B	From a strip of fabric 5½″ × fabric width, use template Tall Duck B to cut 3 *Tall* Duck B triangles.	Trim the strip's width to 4½″. Using template Short Duck B, cut 3 *Short* Duck B triangles.
Template Duck C	From a strip of fabric 6¾″ × fabric width, use template Tall Duck C to cut 3 *Tall* Duck C triangles.	Trim the strip's width to 5¾″. Using template Short Duck C, cut 3 *Short* Duck C triangles.
Template Duck D	From a strip of fabric 3″ × fabric width, use template Tall Duck D to cut 3 *Tall* Duck D triangles.	Trim the strip's width to 2″. Using template Short Duck D, cut 3 *Short* Duck D triangles.

BACKGROUND FABRICS

	Tall templates	Short templates
A background pieces: Cut 24 tall and 24 short.	Cut 5 strips 4¼″ × fabric width. Keep the fabric folded. Use Tall Background A template to cut 2 pairs of pieces from each strip. Open up each strip at the fold and cut 1 additional piece.	Cut 6 strips 3¼″ × fabric width. Use Short Background A template to cut 2 pairs of pieces from each strip.
B background pieces: Cut 24 tall and 24 short.	Cut 5 strips 5½″ × fabric width. Keep the fabric folded. Use Tall Background B template to cut 2 pairs of pieces from each strip. Open up each strip at the fold and cut 1 additional piece.	Cut 6 strips 4½″ × fabric width. Use Short Background B template to cut 2 pairs of pieces from each strip.
C background pieces: Cut 24 tall and 24 short.	Cut 5 strips 6¾″ × fabric width. Keep the fabric folded. Use Tall Background C template to cut 2 pairs of pieces from each strip. Open up each strip at the fold and cut 1 additional piece.	Cut 5 strips 5¾″ × fabric width. Use Short Background C template to cut 2 pairs of pieces from each strip. Open each strip to cut 1 additional piece.
D background pieces: Cut 24 tall and 24 short.	Cut 6 strips 3″ × fabric width. Keep the fabric folded. Use Tall Background D template to cut 2 pairs of pieces from each strip.	Cut 6 strips 2″ × fabric width. Use Short Background D template to cut 2 pairs of pieces from each strip.

PIECE

Ducks to Background Pieces

1. Group background pieces by like template (all background tall A pieces together, all short A pieces together, and so on).

2. For the ducks, sort the triangles in color order within template type. For example, the tall A ducks are sorted into 3 groups, each with a red-orange, orange, yellow, lime, light green, dark green, and teal "duck."

Note: The quilt is made of 24 rows, each with the same size duck. Each row has 7 ducks and 8 background pieces.

3. Working with tall A ducks and tall A background pieces, pin a background piece to a red-orange duck. As it is laid out, make sure the duck is pointing up and the background piece is to the left of the duck. Pin right sides together, matching match points (page 22). Refer to Diagram 1.

4. Sew and press the seams open (Diagram 2).

5. Piece the rest of the background tall A pieces to all tall A ducks.

6. Repeat the process for the remaining tall A as well as the short A, tall B, short B, tall C, short C, tall D, and short D duck and background pieces.

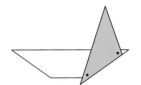

DIAGRAM 1: Pin right sides together.

DIAGRAM 2: Sew background piece to left of duck.

Ducks into Rows

1. Working with tall A ducks, lay out duck-background units in color order with the ducks pointing up and the background pieces on the left side of each duck: red-orange, orange, yellow, lime, light green, dark green, and teal. Add an additional piece to the teal ducks on the right side (Diagram 3).

DIAGRAM 3: Sew background pieces to ducks.

2. Pin and sew the units together into a row. Press the seams open (Diagram 4).

3. Repeat the process to sew all ducks and background pieces into rows (Diagram 5).

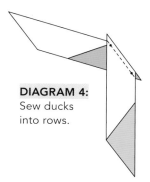

DIAGRAM 4: Sew ducks into rows.

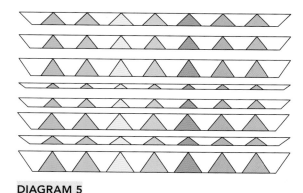

DIAGRAM 5

ASSEMBLE

1. Lay out the 24 rows on a design wall. Configure and experiment with the order of the rows until you're satisfied.

2. Sew the rows together, aligning the centers of the same-colored ducks (Diagram 6).

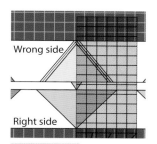

DIAGRAM 6: Align centers of ducks.

For example, the centers of all the orange ducks should be roughly aligned. Use a ruler to help. Also be careful not to nip off the points of the ducks. Press the seams toward bottoms of ducks (Diagram 7).

Finally, trim the left and right sides of the quilt where the extra background pieces jut out. Leave at least a generous ½˝ on each side of the widest duck. You can also choose to leave a couple of inches on either side as I did.

DIAGRAM 7: Quilt assembly

FINISH

Quilt

1. Make a quilt backing 80″ × 102″.

2. Baste the quilt sandwich using your favorite method (see Finishing the Quilt, page 25).

3. Quilt as desired.

4. Trim the backing and batting to the same size as the quilt top. Square the quilt (see Squaring the Quilt, page 27).

Bind

Finish the binding as preferred (see Binding the Quilt, page 27).

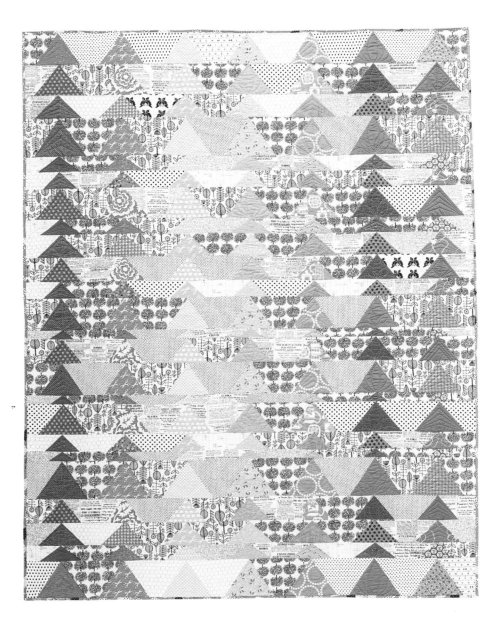

DESIGN IDEA

Personally, I think this quilt would look fantastic using all of the rainbow colors, with the rainbow colors extending into the background pieces, too.

Resizing options: I've provided some sizing options below, but you could also pick and choose the ducks to get the desired quilt length.

	Duck yardage	Background yardage	Cut
Crib quilt 40½″ × 49½″	½ yard each of 4 colors for 6 rows of 4 ducks	2 yards	Cut 8 ducks (2 of each color) from each tall and short B, C, and D duck template. Cut 10 background pieces from each tall and short B, C, and D background template.
Throw quilt 70½″ × 62½″	⅔ yard each of 7 colors for 16 rows of 7 ducks	4 yards	Cut 14 ducks (2 of each color) from each duck template. Cut 16 background pieces from each background template.
Queen-sized quilt 90½″ × 93½″	⅔ yard each of 9 colors for 24 rows of 9 ducks	7 yards	Cut 27 ducks (3 of each color) from each duck template. Cut 30 background pieces from each background template.
King-sized quilt 100½″ × 93½″	⅔ yard each of 10 colors for 24 rows of 10 ducks	7¾ yards	Cut 30 ducks (3 of each color) from each duck template. Cut 33 background pieces from each background template.

IMPROVISATIONAL AND LIBERATED QUILTS

Quilts in this section are a mix of improvisational and liberated quilts. These quilts beg for imperfection and carefree piecing. Forgiving of wonkiness and an "I didn't feel like pinning, so I didn't" approach, they can conform to your style of piecing. In fact, I would say these quilts look better when they are not perfect. Consider the mis-matched seam and the crooked cut to be design elements.

These were among the most challenging quilts I made for this book, both artistically and technically, but they were also some of my favorites. I hope you enjoy making them.

Employing atypical or free-pieced construction, many of these quilts cannot be replicated exactly because of their improvisational nature. Where applicable, though, this section will teach the techniques I used. Generally, listed yardages are estimates and may vary based on your design decisions.

WAVELENGTH

Quilted by Angela Walters

Made from solid fabrics, this improvisational quilt mimics a water-color of graphic triangles. As each triangle overlaps the next, the two colors blend together; this effect adds a layer of mediating color, guiding the rainbow from one side of the quilt to the other.

I will show you the process and provide some guidelines. Then you can make it with your own twist.

Finished Quilt Size: Finished sizes will vary. As shown, 55½″ × 76½″

Materials

RAINBOW FABRICS
- ½ yard of 18 different colors

BACKGROUND FABRICS
- Approximately 5 yards assorted white fabrics

BACKING
- 4¾ yards

BINDING
- ⅝ yard

OTHER MATERIALS
- 64″ × 85″ batting

Cut

You will be making 4 rainbow units: 2 of Rainbow Unit 1 (diamonds pointing to the right) and 2 of Rainbow Unit 2 (diamonds pointing to the left). Typically, a cut of each fabric is enough to make a pair of rainbow units. Cut and piece Rainbow Unit 1 before starting Rainbow Unit 2.

1. Line up the fabrics in color order and pair them. For each pairing, decide which fabric will be the peak triangle and which will be the base triangle.

2. Starting with the pairing that will be at the left, cut strips of equal widths from each pair. Also, for each pair, cut an equal width from the background fabric. For example, cut a strip 4″ × fabric width each from the red-purple, the purple, and the white fabrics.

3. Unfold each fabric strip. Make a cut at 30° near the center of the strip to get 2 pieces of each color (see Cutting at an Angle, page 19) (Diagram 1).

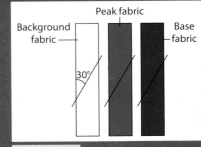

DIAGRAM 1: Cutting first angle

Basic Concept

The basic idea here is to sew rectangular blocks together from fabric widths cut at 30° angles. Once all the blocks are sewn together, the uneven edges are removed from the top and bottom. Sew a couple of test blocks together before cutting all the fabrics.

Strip-Cutting Fundamentals:

- Vary the widths of the strips (between 2″ and 6″).

- Vary the lengths of the peak diamonds (between 2″ and 6″).

- When all the strips are assembled into rainbows, you will cut a straight edge at the bottom of the strips. Any fabric below that line won't be seen.

- The longer the peak diamond (from Step 4), the more peak fabric will show, and the less the base fabric will show.

- As the base fabric gets smaller, the width of the rainbow increases.

- Wider strips of fabric allow for more of the base fabric to show.

- The base triangles tend to drift lower as you work from left to right. If you find the base triangle is too low, cut wider strips for the next pairing.

4. Make a second 30° cut to each peak fabric strip to make it into a diamond shape (Diagram 2).

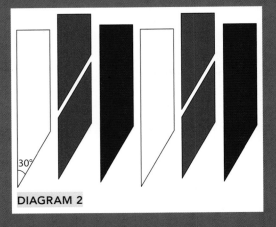

DIAGRAM 2

TIP

Before making the second cut to the peak fabric, I suggest working with a few color pairings at a time on a design surface. Play around with length of the diamond to see how the peaks move. Then cut when satisfied.

5. Repeat Steps 2–4 for all color pairings and background fabric.

6. For the strips on the far left and far right of the rainbow, cut equal widths from each end color. Cut 2 pieces of the same width from the background fabric. Open each strip and make a 30° cut near the center of the strip. Piece a color strip to a background piece. This will yield 2 end pieces from each color. Set aside.

7. Repeat Steps 4–6, using the remaining half from each strip you cut in Step 2 to cut fabric strips to make a second set of rainbow components.

PIECE

Rainbow Unit 1

1. Piece the background, peak, and base pieces into rows. Press the seams open (Diagram 3).

2. Sew the strips together, matching the top right edge of the base piece (A) to the top left edge of the peak diamond (B). Press the seams open (Diagram 4).

3. Continue piecing the rows together in color order. Then sew the end pieces from Cut, Step 6 (page 90) to the left and right sides. Press the seams open (Diagram 5).

4. Repeat Steps 1–3 to sew a second rainbow unit using the remaining half of the cut strips from the first rainbow unit.

Rainbow Unit 2

1. The second set of units will be sewn in mirror image. So flip the rows (compare Diagrams 4 and 6) and work the colors in opposite directions (compare Diagrams 5 and 7). *If you are not using solid fabrics, you'll need to cut the angles in the opposite direction for this set—150°.*

2. Repeat Cut, Steps 2–7 (page 89) and Rainbow Unit 1, Steps 1–4 (above) to sew the 2 rainbow units in mirror image (Diagrams 6 and 7).

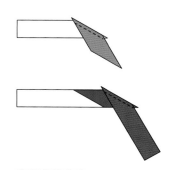

DIAGRAM 3: Piece row.

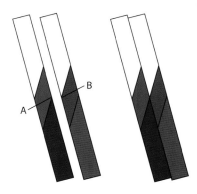

DIAGRAM 4: Piece rows together.

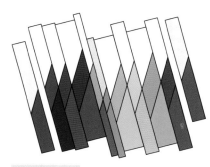

DIAGRAM 5: Add end pieces.

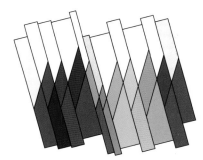

Make 2.

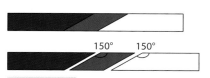

DIAGRAM 6: Piece mirror-image row.

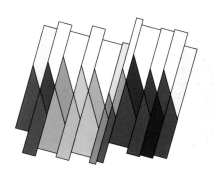

Make 2.

DIAGRAM 7: Piece mirror-image rainbow unit.

Trim

1. Once the rainbow units are pieced, lay them out on a large surface to decide where to trim them.

Place a yardstick or 2 long acrylic rulers across the base of the triangles. To ensure the proper angle, make sure the slant of each triangle is 15° (Diagram 8). If your ruler doesn't have a 15° angle on it, trace the 15° angle pattern (pullout page P1) and tape it to your ruler to use as a guide.

2. Once satisfied with the placement of the cut, trace the line with a fabric-marking pen. Carefully trim along the marked line. I chose to keep the heights of the units roughly the same (18″–19″).

3. Mark and trim the top of the unit as in Steps 1 and 2. Make sure to keep the height of the unit uniform throughout (Diagram 9). (Save trimmed background fabric for Assemble, Step 6, page 93.)

4. Repeat Steps 1–3 for remaining 3 rainbow units.

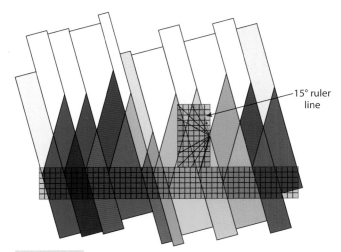

15° ruler line

DIAGRAM 8: Ensuring proper angle before trimming

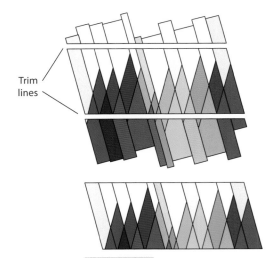

Trim lines

DIAGRAM 9: Trimming rainbow units

ASSEMBLE

1. Lay out the trimmed units, aligning the centers.

2. Measure the longest distance from the edges of the units to the edge of the desired width of the quilt (shown by the arrows in Diagram 10).

3. From the background fabrics, cut strips from the fabric width varying in size from 2˝ to 4˝ and about 2˝ longer than the trimmed height of your rainbow units. Cut enough strips to cover the distance measured in Step 2. Make 8 strip sets, staggering 4 strip sets in 1 direction and the other 4 in the opposite direction. Press the seams open (Diagram 11).

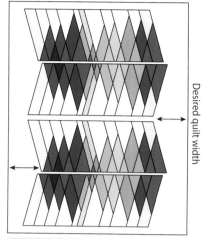

DIAGRAM 10: Measure for background.

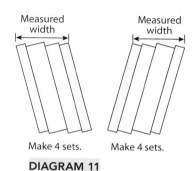

DIAGRAM 11

Make 4 sets. Make 4 sets.

 TIP If the height of the unit is 18˝ or less, you may be able to use half a fabric width (20˝).

4. Sew the background strip sets to the sides of each rainbow unit. Press the seams open. Trim the top and bottom of each strip set (Diagram 12). Repeat this step for all rainbow units.

5. Using the trimmed background fabric (see Trim, Step 3, page 92), cut strips 1½˝ wide. Cut enough strips to cover 2 times the desired quilt width. These will be the narrow horizontal sashing between the rainbow units of the quilt. Sew the strips together end to end to make 2 long strips.

6. Referring to Diagram 13, sew 2 rainbow units to either side of each white 1½˝ strip. Press the seams toward the white strip. Repeat for the other 2 units and white 1½˝ strip.

7. Sew the pairs of rainbow unit pairs together by matching the angled seams in the second and third rainbow units where possible. Press.

8. Square the quilt top.

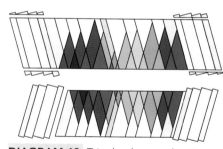

DIAGRAM 12: Trim background units.

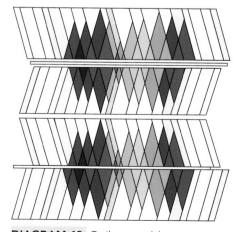

DIAGRAM 13: Quilt assembly

FINISH

Quilt

1. Make a quilt backing and batting that is 4˝ bigger than the quilt top on all sides.

2. Baste the quilt sandwich using your favorite method (see Finishing the Quilt, page 25).

3. Quilt as desired.

4. Trim the backing and batting to the same size as the quilt top. Square the quilt (see Squaring the Quilt, page 27).

Bind

Finish the binding as preferred (see Binding the Quilt, page 27).

RAINBOW REMIX

The artists of Gee's Bend, Alabama, first caught my eye in a book on my mom's coffee table. I think I was still in my sullen teenager phase, when I was too cool for Mom's quilt stuff. But even I couldn't resist Gee's Bend! I found the graphic, simple designs beautiful and sophisticated. The use of color was spectacular.

The Roman Stripes and Roman Stripes variation quilts made by the artists of Gee's Bend inspired *Rainbow Remix*. The characteristic irregular stripes, block sizes, and borders are elements I included in the design of this quilt.

Remember reading about all those techniques at the beginning of this book? Well, forget all that and let's get crazy. Forget the straight lines and right angles, and let's be wonky. But *Rainbow Remix* can be "as wonky as you wanna get." So we'll also discuss ways to adjust the wonk.

Materials

FABRICS

- 1 piece 10″ × 10″ of 50 different-colored solids (or larger pieces if you want larger blocks)

BACKING

- 2½ yards as shown

BINDING

- ½ yard for straight binding or 1 yard for bias binding

OTHER MATERIALS

- 44″ × 56″ batting

Finished Quilt Size: Finished sizes will vary. As shown, approximately 36″ × 48″

Wonk-o-Meter

Let's talk about ways to adjust the wonkiness. As opposed to an either-or, think of each of these categories as a continuum, in which you can dial the wonk up or down within each category.

	More wonky	More classic
Cutting	Use scissors and free cut each strip.	Use rotary cutter and ruler to cut at 90°.
Strip size	Vary length and width of strips.	Keep all strips the same size.
Pressing	Iron blocks using steam to distort them.	Press as usual.
Block size	Vary the block size in length and/or width.	Keep all blocks the same size.
Squaring up the quilt	Keep irregular borders.	Square up as usual.
Technique used for all blocks	Use different wonky techniques in the blocks.	Use the same technique for all blocks.

PIECE

1. Sort the fabrics in color order to make a fabric rainbow. Have fun with the sorting. The colors do not need to be in strict color order. Play with tone, tint, and shade to create variation (see Using the Spectrum in Quilts, page 10).

2. Choose 3 colors that are next to each other in the fabric rainbow. For example, choose a blue-purple, a purple, and a red-purple.

Cut 5 strips from each fabric. I tended to cut strips of the same size from a given fabric, for example skinny strips from the purple, and short and fat strips from the red-purple. Each fabric will be used in 2 blocks (Diagram 1).

DIAGRAM 1: Cut 5 strips from each fabric.

3. Working with 3 strips of the blue-purple and 2 strips of the purple, sew the strips together, sandwiching the 2 strips of purple between the blue-purple strips. Press the seams open. Trim the ends of the blocks so each edge is straight (Diagram 2).

4. Now, working with 3 strips of the purple and 2 strips of the red-purple, sew these strips together, sandwiching the red-purple between the purple. Trim the ends of the blocks so each edge is straight (Diagram 3).

5. Continue making blocks in this manner. For example, the next block would use the remaining 3 red-purple strips with 2 strips of the next color, magenta.

DIAGRAM 2: Blue-purple/purple block

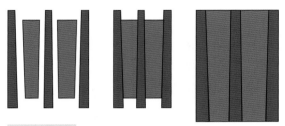

DIAGRAM 3: Purple/red-purple block

ASSEMBLE

1. Once all the blocks are complete, lay them out on a design surface. Arrange them until you're satisfied. Play with the arrangement of color and the direction of the stripes. Leave some blocks out if they don't fit. Keep in mind the final quilt will likely change a bit once everything is all sewn (Diagram 4).

The direction of the stripes generally should rotate 90° with each block—but this quilt isn't a rule follower.

2. Once the arrangement is finalized, think about how best to assemble the quilt using a combination of piecing the blocks into rows and piecing them into larger blocks.

Note: Notice how different the purple looks in these two blocks. This is a great example of color relativity: the same color can appear darker or lighter, and warmer or cooler, depending on the other colors around it.

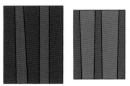

2 blocks

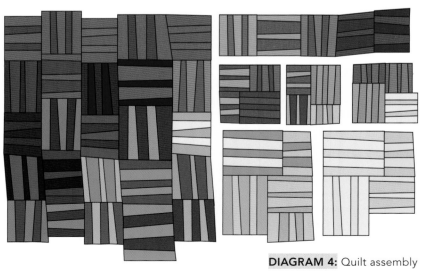

DIAGRAM 4: Quilt assembly

Assembling Rows

1. To join blocks by row, simply sew them together end to end (Diagram 5).

2. If necessary, trim the seam allowances to ¼″ as you piece the blocks (Diagram 6).

3. After each row is finished, trim the edges of each long side so that there is an even edge. The edge doesn't need to be square or straight (Diagram 7).

Assembling Blocks into Bigger Blocks

Another option is to sew groups of blocks into larger blocks.

For example, sew the blocks into pairs. Press. Then sew the pairs into larger units. As in Assembling Rows, above, trim seam allowances and even up edges of blocks as you go (Diagram 8).

DIAGRAM 5: Blocks into rows

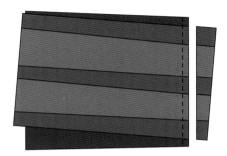

DIAGRAM 6: Trim seam allowances as needed.

DIAGRAM 7: Trim rows.

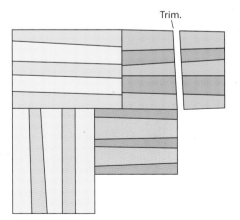

Trim.

DIAGRAM 8: Sew blocks into groups.

FINISH

Quilt

1. Measure the longest width and length of the quilt top. Make a quilt back 4″ larger on each side than the quilt top.

2. Layer the quilt and baste it well using your favorite method (see Finishing the Quilt, page 25).

3. Quilt as desired. I quilted mine with straight lines. First I marked the quilt top with straight lines every ½″ using a Hera marker and an acrylic ruler. Then I quilted the marked lines using a walking foot.

4. Trim the quilt top, back, and batting so that the edges are wonky. Or trim them square (see Squaring the Quilt, page 27).

Bind

1. Make bias binding if the quilt is not square or continuous binding if the quilt is square.

2. Bind using your preferred method (see Binding the Quilt, page 27).

DESIGN IDEAS

Instead of using all colors, choose one neutral to incorporate into each block. A gray neutral paired with different rainbow colors in each block would look lovely.

Or choose a dual color scheme; for example, using variations of blue and green would be pretty.

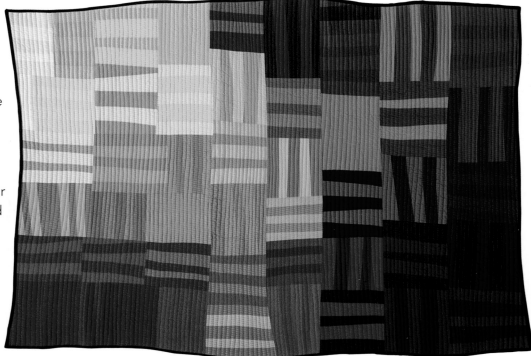

MONSTAR

Two favorites, a rainbow and a star, combine to make a stunning and stellar quilt. (See what I did there?) The star is constructed from spokes made by sewing strips to a 60° diamond. The piecing is similar to piecing Log Cabin blocks.

This is such a fantastic quilt. It's my middle daughter's favorite and it lives on her bed. The quilt can also be sized up for a king- or queen-sized bed quilt by adding a larger background. Decrease the number of star borders to size it down to a baby or throw quilt.

Finished Quilt Size: 80˝ × 92˝

Materials

CENTER STAR FABRICS
- ⅛ yard white for Fabric 1
- ¼ yard beige for Fabric 2

RAINBOW FABRICS
- ¼ yard light pink for Border 1
- ⅓ yard medium pink for Border 2
- ⅓ yard dark pink for Border 3
- ⅜ yard light red for Border 4
- ½ yard dark red for Border 5
- ½ yard yellow for Border 6
- ½ yard lime for Border 7
- ½ yard green for Border 8
- ⅝ yard aqua for Border 9

- ¾ yard teal for Border 10
- ¾ yard blue for Border 11
- ¾ yard purple for Border 12

BACKGROUND FABRICS
- 2⅓ yards extra-wide (108˝) white

BACKING
- 7⅓ yards, or 2½ yards extra-wide (108˝) backing fabric

BINDING
- ¾ yard

OTHER MATERIALS
- 88˝ × 100˝ batting

Cut

CENTER STAR FABRICS
- From Fabric 1, cut a strip 3˝ × fabric width. From the strip, cut 6 diamonds 3˝ wide at 60° (see Cutting Angled Units, page 20).
- From Fabric 2, cut 2 strips 3˝ wide × fabric width. From the strips, cut 6 diamonds 3˝ at 60° and cut 6 strips 5½˝ at 120° (Diagram 1).

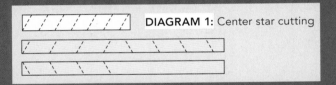
DIAGRAM 1: Center star cutting

TIP

When cutting angled pieces such as diamonds from strips of fabric, you should open up the strip at the fold, cutting one layer at a time.

RAINBOW BORDERS

Color	Border	Number of strips to cut at 2″ × fabric width	Subcut 6 pieces of each of the following sizes (Diagram 2).
Light pink	1	3	5½″ at 60° / 7″ at 120°
Medium pink	2	4	7″ at 60° / 8½″ at 120°
Dark pink	3	4	8½″ at 60° / 10″ at 120°
Light red	4	5	10″ at 60° / 11½″ at 120°
Dark red	5	6	11½″ at 60° / 13″ at 120°
Yellow	6	6	13″ at 60° / 14½″ at 120°
Lime	7	6	14½″ at 60° / 16″ at 120°
Green	8	6	16″ at 60° / 17½″ at 120°
Aqua	9	6	17½″ at 60° / 19″ at 120°
Teal	10	9	19″ at 60° / 20½″ at 120°
Blue	11	12	20½″ at 60° / 22″ at 120°
Purple	12	12	22″ at 60° / 23½″ at 120°

DIAGRAM 2: Example of rainbow border cutting

TIP

Optional: As the borders get longer, you can piece leftover lengths of fabric strips together to save yardage.

PIECE

Press the seams open unless indicated otherwise.

1. Piece center star units: Sew a Fabric 1 (white) 3″ diamond and a Fabric 2 (beige) 3″ diamond together. Press. Piece a 5½″ Fabric 2 strip to this unit. Press. Make 6 (Diagram 3).

2. Piece Border 1 to the center star units by piecing the 60° Fabric 3 (light pink) 5½″-wide strip to the center star unit. Press. Piece a 120° Fabric 3 (light pink) 7½″-wide strip to this unit. Press (Diagram 4).

3. Repeat Step 2 to attach rainbow borders 2–12 to the star unit. Make 6 of these rainbow spokes.

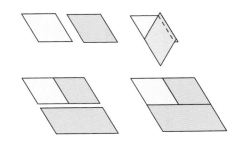

DIAGRAM 3: Piece center star unit.

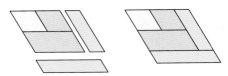

DIAGRAM 4: Begin piecing rainbow borders.

ASSEMBLE

1. Match 2 star points right sides together, pin, and sew. If you plan on turning the edges under for appliqué, start sewing at the center edge and stop sewing ¼″ away from the outer border edge; backstitch (Diagram 5). Press the seams open. Add a third spoke to the 2 you just sewed together.

TIP

After you assemble the star, you'll appliqué it onto the wholecloth quilt top. You can either turn under the edges of the star ¼″ for a neater finish or leave the raw edges unfinished for a more casual look.

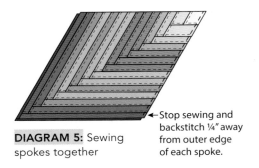

DIAGRAM 5: Sewing spokes together

←Stop sewing and backstitch ¼″ away from outer edge of each spoke.

2. Repeat Step 1 to sew the other half of the star together (Diagram 6).

3. Sew the 2 halves of the rainbow star together, matching the centers. Remember to begin and stop sewing ¼″ away from the outer border edges if you plan on turning the edges under for appliqué. Press.

FINISH

Quilt

1. Press the raw outer edges of the star under ¼″. Prior to making a background and quilt backing, measure the assembled star. It should be approximately 79″ from side to side and 91″ from top to bottom. Make a background 82″ × 94″ and a quilt backing 87″ × 99″. Fold the background into quarters and lightly press to mark center lines.

2. Make a quilt sandwich by layering the quilt backing (right side down), batting (right side up), and quilt top background (right side up). *Spray* baste the quilt sandwich (see Finishing the Quilt, page 25).

3. Position the assembled star on the basted quilt sandwich. Use the center lines as a guide. Spray or pin baste the star (Diagram 7).

4. Quilt as desired and topstitch around the edges of the star.

5. Trim the quilted sandwich to 80″ × 92″, or a little bigger if necessary, making sure to leave at least ½″ of background showing at each star point. Square the quilt (see Squaring the Quilt, page 27).

DIAGRAM 6: Star assembly

DIAGRAM 7: Position star on quilt sandwich.

Bind

Finish the binding as preferred (see Binding the Quilt, page 27).

DESIGN IDEA

Instead of a plain white background, try sewing 4 smaller rectangles of different background fabrics together to make a giant four-patch background. Each rectangle would need to be at least 41¼″ × 46¾″.

This quilt would look great as a scrappy quilt or in a monotone color story.

SIZING

For a baby quilt (43½″ × 50″), sew only up to Border 5. Topstitch the star onto a 51½″ × 58″ quilt sandwich.

For a throw quilt (64″ × 74″), sew only up to Border 9. Topstitch the star onto a 72″ × 81″ quilt sandwich.

For a full-sized or queen-sized quilt, topstitch the 79″ × 91″ star onto an 88″ × 96″ or a 92″ × 101″ quilt sandwich.

ICARUS STAR

Sometimes in life we seem to be running too fast. Taking risks, we have much to do in little time and with a small margin of error. Sometimes we fall. But sometimes we soar.

This quilt, *Icarus Star*, is named for Icarus, the boy who flew too close to the sun. The wings his father made for him fell apart as the wax holding the feathers in place heated in the sun's glory.

This star is made from strip sets pieced into 60° diamonds (see detail, page 109), giving the star a feathered ikat look. The star is then appliquéd off-center onto a plain background.

Finished Quilt Size: 60½˝ × 60½˝

Materials

I chose a scrappy look for this quilt. But the star would look fantastic in a non-scrappy look. If you choose to make the star from yardage (non-scrappy version), the use of one fabric for each color would really make the texture of the star pop. I think solids would look fantastic!

RAINBOW FABRICS

	For a scrappy quilt:	For a non-scrappy quilt:
Red-purples	4 strips 2½˝ × 7˝	⅛ yard
Dark purples	8 strips 2½˝ × 7˝	¼ yard
Teals	12 strips 2½˝ × 7˝	¼ yard
Greens	16 strips 2½˝ × 7˝	⅜ yard
Citrons	20 strips 2½˝ × 7˝	⅜ yard
Oranges	22 strips 2½˝ × 7˝	⅜ yard

STAR BACKGROUND FABRICS

5 grays of varying intensity	For a scrappy quilt:	For a non-scrappy quilt:
Gray 1 (lightest gray)	22 strips 2½˝ × 7˝	⅜ yard
Gray 2	18 strips 2½˝ × 7˝	⅜ yard
Gray 3	14 strips 2½˝ × 7˝	⅓ yard
Gray 4	10 strips 2½˝ × 7˝	¼ yard
Gray 5 (darkest gray)	8 strips 2½˝ × 7˝	¼ yard

QUILT BACKGROUND
- 3½ yards green

BACKING
- 4 yards

BINDING
- ⅝ yard

OTHER MATERIALS
- 2½ yards lightweight nonfusible interfacing, 20˝ wide (or 1⅛ yards, 44˝ wide)
- 69˝ × 69˝ batting

Cut

There are two ways you could cut the rainbow fabrics for this quilt.

RAINBOW FABRICS

Scrappy version
See fabric requirements (page 108) for scrappy cutting.

Non-scrappy version
- From the red-purple, cut 1 strip 2½″ × fabric width. Subcut 2 strips 2½″ × 12″.
- From the dark purple, cut 2 strips 2½″ × fabric width. Subcut 4 strips 2½″ × 12″.
- From the teal, cut 2 strips 2½″ × fabric width. Subcut 6 strips 2½″ × 12″.
- From the green, cut 3 strips 2½″ × fabric width. Subcut 8 strips 2½″ × 12″.
- From the citron, cut 4 strips 2½″ × fabric width. Subcut 10 strips 2½″ × 12″.
- From the orange, cut 4 strips 2½″ × fabric width. Subcut 12 strips 2½″ × 12″.

BACKGROUND FABRICS
- From gray 1, cut 4 strips 2½″ × fabric width. Subcut 12 strips 2½″ × 12″.
- From gray 2, cut 4 strips 2½″ × fabric width. Subcut 10 strips 2½″ × 12″.
- From gray 3, cut 3 strips 2½″ × fabric width. Subcut 8 strips 2½″ × 12″.
- From gray 4, cut 2 strips 2½″ × fabric width. Subcut 6 strips 2½″ × 12″.
- From gray 5, cut 2 strips 2½″ × fabric width. Subcut 6 strips 2½″ × 12″.

PIECE STRIP SETS

Scrappy Version Strip Sets

1. Sew 2½″ × 7″ strips into strip groups. Stagger them so that half are in the same direction and the other half in the opposite direction (refer to Diagram 1). Press the seams open.

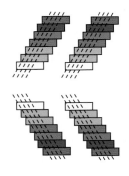

DIAGRAM 1: Cutting scrappy strip sets

Make 4 of each of the following strip sets:

SET A: red-purple / purple / teal / green / citron / orange / gray 1

SET B: purple / teal / green / citron / orange / gray 1 / gray 2

SET C: teal / green / citron / orange / gray 1 / gray 2 / gray 3

SET D: green / citron / orange / gray 1 / gray 2 / gray 3 / gray 4

SET E: citron / orange / gray 1 / gray 2 / gray 3 / gray 4 / gray 5

Make 2 of **SET F:** orange / gray 1 / gray 2 / gray 3 / gray 4 / gray 5 / gray 5

2. Divide the strip sets into 2 groups. Each group should have 11 sets, 2 each of Sets A–E and 1 Set F.

3. From Group 1, subcut the strip sets with grays at the bottom. Cut 3 strips 1½″ at a 60° angle, as shown on the left side of Diagram 1 (refer to Cutting at an Angle, page 19).

4. From Group 2 of the strip sets, with grays at the top, cut 3 strips 1½″ at a 120° angle, as shown on the right side of Diagram 1 (refer to Cutting at an Angle, page 19).

Non-Scrappy Version Strip Sets

1. Sew 2½″ × 12″ strips into strip sets. Stagger the ends of the strips so that half are in the same direction and the other half in the opposite direction (refer to Diagram 2). Press the seams open.

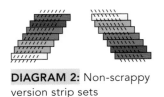

DIAGRAM 2: Non-scrappy version strip sets

Make 2 of each of the following strip sets:

SET A: red-purple / purple / teal / green / citron / orange / gray 1

SET B: purple / teal / green / citron / orange / gray 1 / gray 2

SET C: teal / green / citron / orange / gray 1 / gray 2 / gray 3

SET D: green / citron / orange / gray 1 / gray 2 / gray 3 / gray 4

SET E: citron / orange / gray 1 / gray 2 / gray 3 / gray 4 / gray 5

SET F: orange / gray 1 / gray 2 / gray 3 / gray 4 / gray 5 / gray 5

2. Divide the strip sets into 2 groups. Each group should have a strip from each set, A–F.

3. From Group 1, subcut the strip sets with grays at the bottom. Cut 6 strips 1½˝ at a 60° angle, as shown on the left side of Diagram 1 (refer to Cutting at an Angle, page 19).

4. From Group 2 of strip sets, with grays at the top, cut 6 strips 1½˝ at a 120° angle, as shown on the right side of Diagram 1 (refer to Cutting at an Angle, page 19).

PIECE DIAMONDS

The diamonds will be assembled in this step. The star is composed of 2 groups of 3 diamonds. The groups of diamonds are mirror images of each other, so pay attention to the direction of the angle of the pieces and the colors.

For the first group of diamonds, press the seams toward the gray side. For the other group, press the seams toward the colors.

PIECING TIP

The staggering does not need to be perfect. It's fine to fudge it a bit as a design element. If you prefer a more precise look, it may help to create a midline by folding the strip and finger-pressing it to crease it (Diagram 6). Then match the crease(s) to the seam(s).

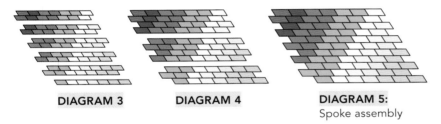

DIAGRAM 3   DIAGRAM 4   DIAGRAM 5:
                                      Spoke assembly

1. From the Group 1 strip sets, sew 2 A strips together, 2 B strips together, 2 C strips together, 2 D strips together, and 2 E strips together. Stagger each pair so that the seams of a strip align with the midpoints (between seams) of the adjacent strip. Press (Diagram 3).

2. Sew A units to B units. Sew C units to D units. Sew E units to F strips. Press (Diagram 4).

3. Sew AB units to CD units. Then sew ABCD units to EF units. See Diagram 3. Press (Diagram 5).

4. Repeat Steps 1–3 to make 2 more similar diamonds. (There will be 3 extra F strips.)

5. Repeat Steps 1–3 with the Group 2 strip sets to create 3 diamonds that are mirror images of the first 3 diamonds (Diagram 7). (There will be 3 extra F strips.)

DIAGRAM 6:
Fold to crease midline of diamond.

DIAGRAM 7

6. Trim the diamonds so that each side is 11½″ long. See Cutting Angled Units (page 20). Refer to Diagrams 8 and 9.

DIAGRAM 8: Group 1 diamonds.

DIAGRAM 9: Group 2 diamonds.

ASSEMBLE

1. Arrange the diamonds in a star, alternating Group 1 and Group 2 diamonds.

2. Sew 3 diamonds together to form half of the star. Repeat with the remaining 3 diamonds. Press the seams open.

3. Sew 2 halves together to form the star. Pin the center seams first and then pin the ends. Pin well between. Stitch the center seam and press open.

4. Cut the interfacing into 2 pieces, each 45″ × 20″. Sew the interfacing pieces along the 45″ edges to create a single piece 45″ × 39½″. Leave a 5″ opening in the middle seam for turning later on.

5. Lay the star on top of the interfacing (right sides together) and pin all the way around. Stitch ¼″ from the edges of the star. Trim the excess interfacing around the star (Diagram 10).

6. Trim the extra fabric from the points in the star (Diagram 11). Turn the star right side out using a chopstick, unsharpened pencil, or other blunt turning tool. Press.

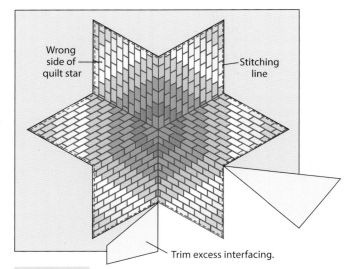

Wrong side of quilt star

Stitching line

Trim excess interfacing.

DIAGRAM 10: Sew interfacing to star.

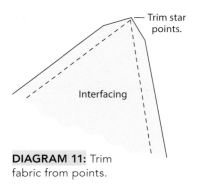

Trim star points.

Interfacing

DIAGRAM 11: Trim fabric from points.

7. Make a background 60½″ × 60½″.

8. Position the star as desired on the background fabric (Diagram 12). Pin in place. Topstitch ⅛″ from the edges of the star.

FINISH

Quilt

1. Make a quilt backing 69″ × 69″.

2. Layer and baste the quilt sandwich using your favorite method (see Finishing the Quilt, page 25).

3. Quilt as desired.

4. Trim the backing and batting to the same size as the quilt top. Square the quilt (see Squaring the Quilt, page 27).

Bind

Finish the binding as preferred (see Binding the Quilt, page 27).

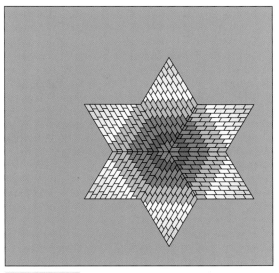

DIAGRAM 12: Position star on background.

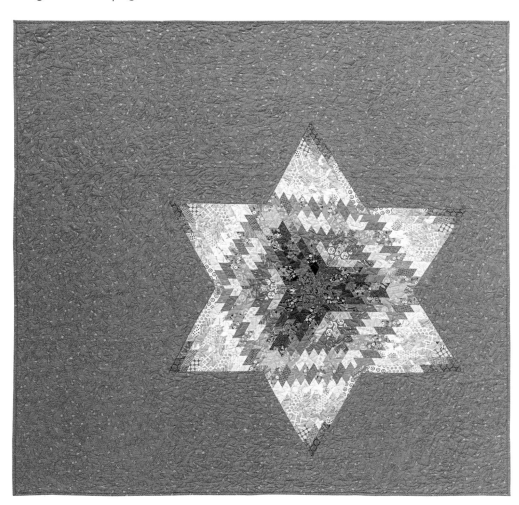

THE IMPOSSIBLE RAINBOW

Quilted by Angela Walters

Without light, a rainbow cannot exist. Playing on that idea, this quilt features a rainbow at night—a paradoxical thing.

This quilt is made in the spirit of liberated quiltmaking. Typically, the goal in piecing is to make each point match, perfectly. My intention here was to avoid matching the points, but I didn't want to clip the points off, so they remain crisp and sharp in the quilt. So I staggered the intersections of points. I feel this gives the colors the effect of floating.

As you make this quilt, have fun. Keep in mind that as you piece the units together, the colored center squares will drift a bit to the right.

Finished Quilt Size: Finished sizes will vary. As shown, 60″ × 75″

Materials

RAINBOW FABRICS
- ⅛ yard (or scraps) of 24 different colors

BACKGROUND FABRICS
- Approximately 5¾ yards black shot cotton

BACKING
- Approximately 4⅔ yards

BINDING
- ⅝ yard

OTHER MATERIALS
- 68″ × 83″ batting

Cut

RAINBOW FABRICS

1. From each of the 24 colors, cut 7 squares ranging in size from 1¾″ to 3″ (see chart, at right). I cut squares at 1¾″, 2″, 2¼″, 2½″, 2¾″, and 3″. Cut a total of 168 squares.

2. Arrange the colored squares into piles by size. Count how many squares are in each pile, and record the numbers in the chart. I have noted how many are in my quilt.

	1¾″	2″	2¼″	2½″	2¾″	3″
Number of squares (my version)	38	35	19	23	22	31
Number of squares (your version)						

BACKGROUND FABRICS

Each colored square needs a 17″ strip of background fabric. For example, if you cut 38 colored squares 1¾″, cut 38 background strips 1¾″ × 17″. Then you will subcut each background strip in half so that each square has a left- and right-side strip.

Let's talk about the easiest way to do the cutting using the 38 squares 1¾″ as an example (Diagram 1).

1. From the black yardage, cut 1 strip 17″ × fabric width.

2. From the strip, subcut 22 strips 1¾″ × 17″.

3. Then subcut each strip in half so that each measures 1¾″ × 8½″.

4. Repeat until you've cut enough strips 1¾″ × 17″ to equal the number of 1¾″ squares (38 squares and 38 strips).

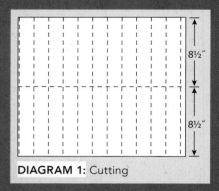

DIAGRAM 1: Cutting

5. Continue cutting 17″ strips of background fabric, cutting a strip for each square. The strip width should be exactly the same as the width of the squares: 1¾″, 2″, 2¼″, 2½″, 2¾″, or 3″.

PIECE

1. Sew an 8½″-long strip to opposite sides of the square to make a unit. Press the seam open (Diagram 2). Repeat for each square to make a total of 168 units (Diagram 3).

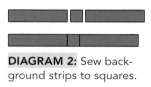

DIAGRAM 2: Sew background strips to squares.

2. Sort the units into 7 groups of 24 units. Each group gets a unit of each color. To vary the column sizes, distribute the sizes of squares unequally (for example, put more small squares in a column). You can either sort the units into groups, by color, without regard to size, or sort them deliberately using a design wall.

DIAGRAM 3: Units of varying size

3. Piece the units together in color order. As you sew the units together, stagger the strip ends so the squares align vertically. Press the seams open. I chose not to align some of my points so that the squares would appear to float (Diagram 4).

4. Sew 7 columns with 24 colors each. You may choose to leave some colors out here and there for added interest.

TIP Sew the units together into pairs and then into groups of four, and so on. I find this more manageable than adding units one at a time.

5. Trim each column to remove jagged edges and so that columns are the same width throughout. The widths may vary, but they should be around 10″–12″ wide (Diagram 5).

Note: Depending on how much you stagger the units, you will notice that the trimming line is a bit slanted. The key here is to keep the width consistent throughout the column.

ARRANGE

On a design wall, lay out the columns. Arrange them until you're satisfied, moving some columns up and others down.

Cutting the Background Pieces

1. Measure the width of each column. Then measure the longest distance between where the quilt top will end and the column. For demonstration purposes let's say a column measures 11½″ and the longest distance between where the quilt top will end and the column is 18″ (Diagram 6).

> **TIP**
>
> Mom always said: It's easier to cut bigger and trim down. After measuring for the background pieces for each column, cut pieces longer than the measurements. Once all the columns are sewn together, you can trim the ends as needed.

2. From the background fabric, cut a strip 11½″ × 19″ (or longer) and then cut a 45° angle from lower left to upper right at the left end of the strip.

3. Repeat Steps 1 and 2 for the top of this column and for both the top and the bottom of each of the other 6 columns.

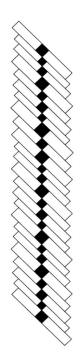

DIAGRAM 4: Arrange units in rainbow order and piece into columns.

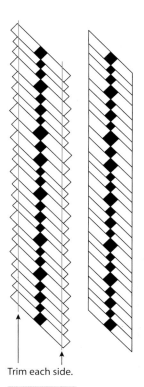

Trim each side.

DIAGRAM 5: Trim sides of each column.

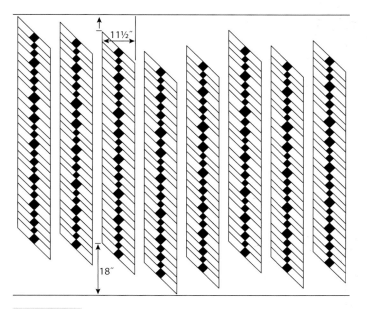

11½″

18″

DIAGRAM 6: Measure for background pieces.

ASSEMBLE

1. Sew the background triangles to each column. Press. Trim if necessary (Diagram 7).

2. Sew columns together. Press (Diagram 8).

FINISH

Quilt

1. Make a quilt backing 4″ bigger than the quilt top on all sides.

2. Layer the quilt sandwich and baste well using your preferred method (see Finishing the Quilt, page 25).

3. Quilt as desired.

4. Trim the backing and batting to the same size as the quilt top. Square the quilt (see Squaring the Quilt, page 27).

Bind

Bind using the method preferred (see Binding the Quilt, page 27).

DESIGN IDEA

My initial inspiration for this quilt was an antique quilt (not an unusual source of inspiration). For a more traditional quilt, cut squares that are all the same size. Maybe 2½″ squares from a jelly roll? Then cut background strips 2½″ × 17″.

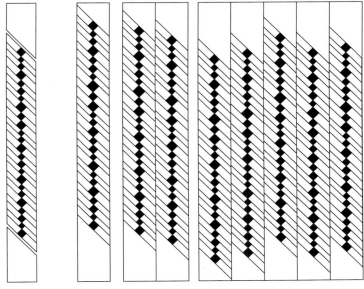

DIAGRAM 7: Sew background pieces to columns.

DIAGRAM 8: Quilt assembly

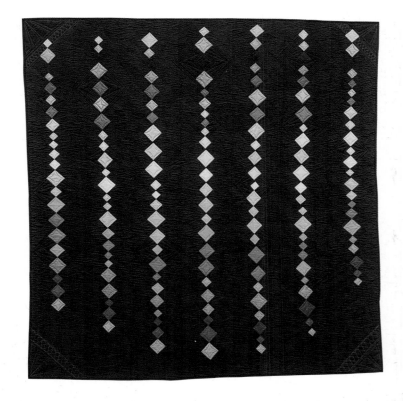

ABOUT THE AUTHOR

As a fourth-generation quilter, Rebecca grew up in a family of makers. Her lovely mother graciously taught her everything she knew about sewing and helped Rebecca make her first official quilt for her first official apartment. Rebecca has been quilting passionately ever since.

Once upon a time, Rebecca taught high school, earned a master's degree, and worked in research. Back then she found her creative outlet in embroidery and quiltmaking. These days every bit of Rebecca's education and mental energy goes toward raising her young children—as only a perfectionist and overachiever would—but she still finds her creative outlet in designing and making quilts.

Rebecca lives in Houston, Texas, with her husband, four children, and two dogs. You can find out more about Rebecca and her quilts by visiting her blog, www.bryanhousequilts.com.

Photo by Amanda Faucett

stash BOOKS®

fabric arts for a handmade lifestyle

If you're craving beautiful authenticity in a time of mass-production...Stash Books is for you. Stash Books is a line of how-to books celebrating fabric arts for a handmade lifestyle. Backed by C&T Publishing's solid reputation for quality, Stash Books will inspire you with contemporary designs, clear and simple instructions, and engaging photography.

ctpub.com